WISDOM OF THE EAST

# LEGENDS OF INDIAN BUDDHISM

WISDOM OF THE EAST

# LEGENDS OF INDIAN BUDDHISM

TRANSLATED FROM "L'INTRODUCTION A L'HISTOIRE DU BUDDHISME INDIEN" OF EUGENE BURNOUF

WITH INTRODUCTION BY
WINIFRED STEPHENS

EUGENE BURNOUF

GYAN

*Published by*

Gyan Publishing House
5, Ansari Road
Daryaganj, New Delhi-110002
Phone: 011-47034999, 9811692060
E-mail: books@gyanbooks.com

*Distribution Network*
gyanbooks.com
India, USA, Canada, UK, Australia, France



ISBN : 978-81-212-3697-3 (PB)
First Published, 1911

2nd Impression 2020

*Printed at:* Gyan Press, Delhi.



**Legends of Indian Buddhism**
Author: Eugene Burnouf

WISDOM OF THE EAST

# LEGENDS OF INDIAN BUDDHISM

TRANSLATED FROM "L'INTRODUCTION À L'HISTOIRE DU BUDDHISME INDIEN" OF EUGENE BURNOUF

WITH INTRODUCTION BY

WINIFRED STEPHENS

Wer sich selbst und And're kennt
Wird auch hier erkennen:
Orient und Occident
Sind nicht mehr zu trennen.

LONDON

JOHN MURRAY, ALBEMARLE STREET, W.

1911

# CONTENTS

# EDITORIAL NOTE

THE object of the Editors of this series is a very definite one. They desire above all things that, in their humble way, these books shall be the ambassadors of good-will and understanding between East and West—the old world of Thought and the new of Action. In this endeavour, and in their own sphere, they are but followers of the highest example in the land. They are confident that a deeper knowledge of the great ideals and lofty philosophy of Oriental thought may help to a revival of that true spirit of Charity which neither despises nor fears the nations of another creed and colour. Finally, in thanking press and public for the very cordial reception given to the "Wisdom of the East" Series, they wish to state that no pains have been spared to secure the best specialists for the treatment of the various subjects at hand.

L. CRANMER-BYNG.
S. A. KAPADIA.

NORTHBROOK SOCIETY,
21 CROMWELL ROAD,
KENSINGTON, S.W.

# LEGENDS OF INDIAN BUDDHISM

## INTRODUCTION

AMONG the many religious beliefs originating in the speculative Oriental mind, Buddhism is one which becomes increasingly attractive to Occidentals. Dissatisfied with the system of rewards and punishments mitigated by sacrifice and mercy, to which the race has so long been enslaved, the modern mind of the West is inclined to favour a creed which teaches that good inevitably brings forth good, and evil evil.

In the number of its adherents and in the area of its prevalence Buddhism surpasses any other creed; and its existence through twenty-four centuries entitles it to be considered one of the most venerable forms of belief.

Buddhism in its purity ignored the existence of a God it denied the existence of a soul; it was not so much a religion as a code of ethics. The relations of Buddhism to the still more ancient religion of Hinduism may be compared to the relation of Christianity to Judaism. As Christians saw in Christianity the fulfilment of Judaism, so Buddhists beheld in their creed the natural evolution of Hinduism. It has been maintained[1] that Buddhism, while introducing into the older religion several striking innovations, involved no absolute break with Hinduism. As Jesus was born and brought up a Jew, so was Gautama,[2] the founder of Buddhism, born and brought up a Hindu. As certain pagan myths and pagan festivals became Christianised, so, in a much greater degree, did Hindu mythology pass into Buddhist legends. Gautama, we are told, came to deliver not men only, but the deities, or devas, of Hinduism. We read that "to the city of deliverance he led thousands of men and gods," that "to eighty thousand divinities he revealed the truth."

In the Buddhist as in the Homeric world,

[1] See Renan, *Nouvelles Etudes d'histoire Religieuse* (1884), p. 159, and Dr. L. D. Barnett, *The Path of Light* (Wisdom of the East Series), Introduction, p. 8. To Dr. Barnett and to Mrs. Bode the present writer wishes to express her gratitude for the reading of the MS. of this work and for useful suggestions, which she has been happy to adopt.

[2] Gautama was the family name of the Buddha, or Enlightened One (see Heinrich Kern, *Der Buddhismus und seine Geschichte in Indien*, 1882, vol. i. p. 313). At his birth, *circ.* 560 B.C. (*ibid.*, p. 36), he received the name of Siddhârtha, which means "he who has accomplished his aim." His disciples called him by numerous titles, many of which will appear in these pages.

gods and men lived side by side. Indeed, the deities of both worlds are but beings living under happier conditions than men.

Gautama seems to have accepted not Hindu mythology only, but the Hindu theory of the universe. At any rate he appears to have made no attempt to formulate any theory of his own. But long after his death, his disciples, according to their various schools of philosophy,[1] evolved theories which they attributed to Gautama. One of these is expressed in a dialogue[2] between Gautama and his disciple Kâśyapa.

"On what doth the earth repose, O Gautama?" asked Kâśyapa.

"The earth reposeth on the circle of the waters, O Brahman."

"And the circle of the waters, on what doth it repose?"

"It reposeth on the wind."

"And the wind, O Gautama, on what doth it repose?"

"It reposeth on the ether."

"And the ether, O Gautama, on what reposeth it?"

"Thou searchest too far, O great Brahman,

[1] E. Burnouf in *L'Introduction à l'Histoire du Buddhisme Indien* (1876, p. 397) says there were four chief schools founded by the four chief disciples of Gautama—Rahula his son, Kâśyapa, Upâli, and Kâty-ây-ana.

[2] *Ibid.*, p. 400.

thou searchest too far. The ether, O Brahman, reposeth on nothing; it hath no support."

We Occidentals, however, are not likely to go to Buddhism for any system of physics or of metaphysics. The attraction of Gautama's teaching for Western minds lies in his theory of good and evil, and in the rules for conduct which he laid down. And there is no doubt that in the past his doctrine has exerted a great civilising and humanising influence, first in that north-eastern corner of India where he lived[1] and worked, then throughout the Indian Peninsula, and later in eastern lands beyond India.

The way of salvation preached by Gautama is in effect a system of intellectual and moral self-culture. It depends not upon the mediation of any god or priest, not upon the offering of any sacrifice or any mortification of the flesh, not upon the accomplishment of any outward act, but upon the growth of the inner nature to be brought about by self-control and diligence. Every man must "be a lamp unto himself, to hold fast . . . to the truth, to look not for refuge to any one besides himself."

The reformed creed of Gautama involved a

[1] He was born of the Śâkya tribe, in the grove of Lumbini, not far from his father's city of Kapilavastu. Aśoka's original empire was that of Magadha, situated immediately south of the Ganges. But he extended his dominion over vast areas, from the valley of Cabul to the mouths of the Ganges and from the Himalayas to south of the Vindhya mountains.

certain modification of the older Hindu doctrines. Perhaps the most striking innovation it introduced was its rejection of the caste system. The greatest Buddhist King, the Aśoka of these legends, was following his master, Gautama, when he said of Buddha's Law:

"Caste may be considered when it is a question of marriage or of an invitation, but not of the Law, for the Law's fulfilment is the result of virtue, and virtue dependeth not upon caste. . . . For the sage there is no difference between the body of a prince and the body of a slave."[1]

Gautama's rejection of penance as a means of salvation was another deviation from Hinduism. It was one which the devotees of the older religion found great difficulty in accepting. When the Brahmans beheld Buddhist monks wearing fine linen and reclining on soft couches they doubted their sincerity.[2]

Hindus were probably readier to accept the fundamental truths of Buddhism. The all-important Buddhist doctrine of Karma was, indeed, a modification of the Hindu belief in the transmigration of souls; and closely associated with Karma was the belief in the eight-fold path to deliverance or salvation and the final attainment of deliverance in Nirvâṇa.

Denying, as he did, the existence of the soul,

[1] 'The Establishment of the Law by Aśoka,' see *post*, p. 47.

[2] Legend of Vītaśoka, see *post*, p. 101.

it was impossible for Gautama to accept the theory of the soul's transmigration. He substituted for it the doctrine of transmigration of character, or the doctrine of Karma. Karma has been described as the moral power working in the universe. Gautama held that after the death of any being, human, animal, or divine, "there survived nothing at all save the being's 'Karma,' the result, that is, of that being's mental and bodily actions. Every creature is the last inheritor and the last result of the Karma of a long series of past creatures—a series so long that its beginning is beyond the reach of calculation, and its end will be coincident with the destruction of the world." Hence every action, mental or physical, good or evil, somewhere in the course of time has its reward or its retribution: evil produces evil, good produces good with eternal inevitability. No exterior power, no mortification of the flesh, no priestly or personal sacrifice can destroy the fruit of a man's deeds. His actions must work out their full effect to the pleasant or to the bitter end. The reward or the retribution may be delayed for ages, at length it is bound to come. "Works are not destroyed by hundreds of Kalpas (ages); but when in due time deeds have attained their consummation they bring forth fruits for creatures endowed with bodies."[1] "Man dies and passes

[1] 'The Eyes of Kuṇâla,' see *post*, p. 79.

away; but, by means of a certain yearning for life, which every ordinary man feels, his good or evil *karma* (literally his 'doing') does not die: a new being is produced in a more or less painful and material state of existence, according to the desert or merit of the being who had died."[1]

Three legends in this volume forcibly illustrate the doctrine of Karma: the story of King Aśoka's son, Kuṇâla; of Kuṇâla's contemporary, Sundara; and of Aśoka's brother, Vîtaśoka. In Kuṇâla's case, beauty and royal rank are the reward of his restoration, in a previous existence, of a ruined Buddhist temple, while the loss of his eyes befalls him as retribution for his having, in a former life, blinded a herd of gazelles. In like manner, for deeds performed in earlier stages of existence did Sundara and Vîtaśoka suffer punishment and enjoy reward.

From such inevitability of cause and effect Gautama taught that there exists one way of escape. A narrow path it is, and few there be that find it. Yet the few, who are most blessed, may pass through seven stages and attain at length deliverance, Nirvâṇa, the state of perfect knowledge. The seven stages lead from contemplation to greater and greater wisdom—that is, to purer and purer detachment from the world, until in perfect wisdom all craving for

[1] Rhys Davids, *Manual of Buddhism* (1894), pp. 103, 104.

existence vanishes. Then and then only the Karma ceases to be individualised, personality is extinguished, and Nirvâṇa is attained.

Few indeed are the creatures who attain to the last stage in the eightfold path. Gautama and the twenty-four other Buddhas who preceded him have entered into Nirvâṇa, but only after countless ages of heroic struggle in many different births. Not one of the heroes whose progress towards deliverance is related in the following legends attains this consummation.

The six legends of this volume are translated from *L'Introduction à l'Histoire du Buddhisme Indien*, by Eugène Burnouf, one of those great Frenchmen to whose labours in the early nineteenth century the Western world largely owes its knowledge of this venerable creed.

But Burnouf could never have carried out his researches had it not been for the Englishman, Brian Houghton Hodgson.[1] During his twenty-three years' residency in Nepāl, from 1820 until 1843, Hodgson unearthed from Buddhist monasteries an invaluable collection of Buddhist manuscripts in the Sanskrit tongue. These he bestowed on the Asiatic societies of Calcutta, London, and Paris. And it is on the Paris collection of those documents, in which, says Burnouf, we probably possess the very foundation

[1] See Sir William Wilson Hunter, *Life of Brian Houghton Hodgson* (1896).

of the vast system of Buddhism, that *L'Introduction à l'Histoire du Buddhisme Indien* is based.

Since Burnouf's day extensive researches have been made among the Buddhist inscriptions and in the Buddhist temples of India, and much still remains to be done; yet the work of the great French scholar, who was one of the pioneers of this study, has never been superseded.

The Sanskrit documents discovered by Hodgson and used by Burnouf are of a date considerably posterior to the fifth century B.C., when Gautama is said to have lived. In addition to the teaching of the Buddha's own discourses, these documents present an elaborate system of religious discipline and metaphysics, which was evolved by his disciples. Hence in the following legends the beautiful morality and the rich spirituality of Gautama's gospel will be found frequently overlaid by the accretions of crude polytheism and fantastic superstition.

From among the legends reproduced by Burnouf these stories have been selected for various reasons: first, as illustrating fundamental Buddhist doctrines; second, as revealing the civilising influence of Buddhism; and last, as telling the history of Aśoka, that greatest among Buddhist kings, who reigned in the second century before Christ.[1]

[1] The Cingalese and other Buddhists believe that there was an earlier Aśoka who reigned about one hundred years

"Wherever the teaching of the Buddha has spread, from the Volga to Japan, from Ceylon and Siam to the borders of Mongolia and Siberia, the name of King Aśoka is known and reverenced."

In the early years of his reign Aśoka was a great warrior and a great conqueror. Then, about ten years after his accession, according to the King's own account contained in his thirteenth edict,[1] he realised the horrors of war, and became convinced that the only true conquest was conquest by religion. It has been suggested[2] that in his conversion Aśoka, like Constantine, was actuated by considerations of state, that the Indian king, like the Roman emperor, was impressed by the high organisation of the religion he adopted, as well as by the noble characters of its adherents. This, however, is pure hypothesis.

According to legend Aśoka was converted by a miracle[3] in the tenth year of his reign.

after Gautama (see *post*, 'The Eyes of Kuṇāla,' p. 99, note). Burnouf's narratives of Aśoka are taken from the Aśoka Avadāma, in Buddhist Sanskrit, preserved in Nepāl. Other narratives dealing with the great King are to be found in the Pāli Mahāvamsa, preserved in Ceylon, and in Buddaghosa's account in his commentary on the *Vinaya* (Rhys Davids, *Buddhist India*, 1903, p, 276).

[1] See *post*, p. 17, and 'The Conversion of Aśoka,' p. 39, note.

[2] Edmund Hardy, *Kōnig Aśoka* (1902), p. 30, and Rhys Davids, *Indian Buddhism*, p. 298.

[3] See *post*, 'The Conversion of King Aśoka,' pp. 38-40.

From Aśoka the Furious or Chandaśoka, he was transformed into Dharmaśoka or the Aśoka of the Law. The warrior who had spread devastation and murder throughout India began to engage in works of peace, in making roads, in digging wells and planting trees, in establishing charities and providing for their businesslike distribution. Many were the great monasteries and temples built by the converted Aśoka. Throughout the vast dominions which his conquests had added to his original empire of Magadha, on pillars and on rocks he engraved the articles of Buddhist belief. These inscriptions are described as edicts. They are the only known contemporary documents for the history of Aśoka's reign and for the study of his religion.

By means of these edicts and by means of missionaries Aśoka is said to have extended Buddhism throughout India. From a great council held at Pâṭaliputtra,[1] in 250 B.C., he is said to have sent forth missionaries to all parts of India, and even to countries outside the Indian peninsula—to Ceylon, and possibly to Thibet.

At this Council of Pâṭaliputtra, Aśoka would seem to have established the cause of sacred Buddhist writings, as well as certain articles of Buddhist faith. In the Council's decrees, a recent Italian writer discerns, some five centuries

[1] The modern Patna.

before the Christian Edict of Milan, the earliest trace of a principle of religious liberty.[1]

Religious toleration is likewise the theme of one of Aśoka's rock edicts, wherein the King decrees that no one shall disparage other sects in order to exalt his own, and that honour shall be paid to the followers of other religions. After a reign of some forty-six years, from about 268 to 222 B.C., Aśoka died great and fortunate. His glory, it was believed, would endure as long as the Law of Buddha, which he had so strictly observed and so powerfully propagated.

The creed of Aśoka was Buddhism in its purity. Under his sway the law of Buddha and the organisation of his religion attained its highest development. After Aśoka's death the history of India and of the Buddhist belief in India is somewhat obscure. It has yet to be deciphered from untranslated inscriptions and manuscripts. Two facts, however, are established, viz. that some centuries after Aśoka's death Buddhism was rapidly decaying throughout India, and that this decline continued until not a single Buddhist remained in the land where Buddhism arose. The precise causes of the disappearance of Buddhism from India are as yet undetermined.[2] It has been suggested that

[1] L. Luzzatti, *Liberté de Conscience et Liberté de Science*, trad. par J. Chamard (Paris, 1900), pp. 71 *et passim*.

[2] See A. Barth, *Religions of India* (1882), pp. 133–138.

Aśoka's munificent gifts to the order of Buddhist monks, by fostering a corrupt and worldly spirit among the disciples of the Master, contributed to the expulsion of his faith from the land of its birth.

> Truth fails not; but her outward forms that bear
> The longest date do melt like frosty rime,
> That in the morning whiten'd hill and plain
> And is no more.

WINIFRED STEPHENS.

*London*, 1911.

# I

## THE CHILDHOOD AND YOUTH OF AŚOKA

AND in those days King Bimbisâra[1] reigned in the city of Râjagṛiha. The son of Bimbisâra was Ajâtaśatru. And Ajâtaśatru begat Ujjâyin; and Ujjâyin begat Munda; and Munda begat Sahâlin; and Sahâlin begat Tulakuchi; and Tulakuchi begat Mahâmaṇḍala; and Mahâmaṇḍala begat Prasenajit; and Prasenajit begat Nanda; and the son of Nanda was Bindusâra. King Bindusâra reigned in the city of Pâṭaliputtra. He had a son whose name was Susîma.

Now in those days, in the city of Champâ was a Brahman, the father of a fair and amiable daughter, who became the pride of the country. At her birth the astrologers had made the following prediction: "This child shall espouse a king and shall give birth to two jewels of sons: one shall be a king,

[1] Bimbisâra was a contemporary of the Buddha.

Chakravartin,[1] master of the four quarters of the earth; the other, after having embraced a religious life, shall behold the fruit of his good works."

Having heard this prophecy, the Brahman was transported with joy, for man ever loveth prosperity. Taking his daughter with him, he repaired to Pâṭaliputtra. In this city he adorned her with all manner of beautiful ornaments, and then gave her to King Bindusâra to be his wife, saying: "Behold, O King, a fortunate maiden and a perfect." Then did King Bindusâra place her in the inner apartments of his palace. There the King's women reflected: "Lo! here is a charming woman, ravishing to look upon; she is the pride of her country, and if the King take her unto himself, he will never look at us again." Wherefore they taught her the trade of a barber; and the Brahman's daughter began to dress the King's hair and his beard, so that she became skilled at the work. . . . One day, when the King was pleased with her, he asked her what favour she desired.

"My Lord," replied the girl, "let the King consent to take me to wife."

"But thou art of the barbers' caste," objected

[1] . . . A prince of earthly dominance,
A Chakravartin, such as rise to rule,
Once in each thousand years.
EDWIN ARNOLD, *The Light of Asia.*

Bindusâra, "and I, the royal anointed, am of the race of the Shattriyas. How is it possible for me to take thee to wife?"

"I am not of the barbers' caste," she replied; "I am the daughter of a Brahman, who gave me unto the King to be his wife."

"Then who hath taught thee the barbers' craft?" inquired the King.

"The women of the inner apartments; and I am resolved never more to exercise that craft," she replied.

In the end the King recognised her as the first of his wives. And she conceived, and in due time brought forth a son. When the festival of his birth had been celebrated with great magnificence, the Queen was asked: "What shall be the name of the child?" And she answered: "At his birth I suffered no pangs (aśoka), wherefore let the child's name be Aśoka," which, being interpreted, meaneth "griefless." Thereafter she bore a second son; and because at his birth also the Queen did not suffer, he was named Vîgataśoka or Vîtaśoka, which being interpreted meaneth "one from whom grief is far away."

Aśoka's limbs were hard to the touch; wherefore he was not pleasing unto the King Bindusâra. On a day, the King desirous to put his sons to the test, summoned the mendicant Pingala vatsâjîva and said unto him:

"Let us put these children to the test, O master, in order that we may know which of them is able to be king when I shall be no more."

Then the mendicant Pingala vatsâjîva replied: "O King, take thy children to the garden in which is the golden mandara,[1] and there we will put them to the test." The King took his children and went into the garden, where was the golden mandara. Meanwhile the Queen said to the young Aśoka: "The King is putting his children to the test; he hath gone to the garden where is the golden mandara; you must go also." "I do not please the King," replied Aśoka; "he will not even look at me; what good is it for me to go?" "Go nevertheless," said his mother. Then said Aśoka, "Send some food before me."

Aśoka went forth from the town Pâṭaliputtra, which was his father's capital. . . . As he went he saw an old elephant which had once carried the King. Aśoka mounted the elephant and rode to the garden of the golden mandara where he alighted among the children and sat upon the ground. The children then received their food. For Aśoka the Queen had sent rice and curds in an earthen vessel.

Then King Bindusâra thus addressed the mendicant Pingala vatsâjîva: "Put the children to

[1] A lovely flower with a sweet fragrance.

the test, O master, in order that I may see who among them is able to reign after me."

Pingala vatsâjîva began to look at the children and to meditate: "Aśoka is he that shall be king," he thought to himself; "and yet he findeth not favour with the King. If I say Aśoka shall be king I shall be in danger of my life."

Then the mendicant opened his mouth and spoke: "O King, I shall make my prediction without distinction of persons."

"Do so," said the King.

The mendicant continued: "He who hath a fine steed, sire, shall be king."

And each of the children thought to himself: "I have a fine steed; I shall be king."

Aśoka reflected: "I came on the back of an elephant, I have a fine steed; therefore I shall be king."

Then said Bindusâra: "Continue the test, O master."

Pingala vatsâjîva opened his mouth and spoke: "O King, he who hath the best seat shall be king."

And each one of the children thought: "I have the best seat." Aśoka reflected: "The earth is my seat; it is I who shall be king." Likewise did the mendicant take for a sign the food and the drink of the children and the vessel in which their food was contained. Then, having spoken, he departed.

The Queen said unto her son: "Which of the King's sons hath been appointed to be king?"

"The prophecy was made without distinction of persons," replied Aśoka. "In this manner: he whose steed, whose seat, whose vessel, whose drink, and whose food is the best, he shall be king. If I mistake not, it is I who shall be king. For my steed was the elephant's back, my seat was the earth, my vessel an earthen pot, my food rice seasoned with curds, and my drink water."

Then the mendicant began to pay his addresses to Aśoka's mother. Wherefore one day she said unto him: "O master, which of my two sons shall be king on the death of Bindusâra?"

"Aśoka shall be king," answered the mendicant.

Then said the Queen unto him: "It might come to pass that the King might question thee with a persistency which thou couldest not evade. Depart therefore from this country and take refuge beyond the frontier. When thou hearest that Aśoka is king, then mayest thou return."

Wherefore the mendicant departed and sought refuge beyond the frontier.

Thereafter King Bindusâra desired to lay siege to the town of Takshaśilâ. Thither he sent his son Aśoka, saying unto him: "Go, my son, and lay siege to the town of Takshaśilâ."

But the King, albeit he gave him an army of four divisions, refused him arms and chariots.

When the young Aśoka sallied forth from Pâṭaliputtra, his followers remonstrated with him, saying: "Prince, we have no weapons; wherewithal shall we fight?"

Then Aśoka cried out, saying:

"If there be within me any virtue which as it ripeneth shall win me the throne, then let men and weapons appear!"

Hardly had the Prince spoken when the earth opened and the Devatâs[1] brought unto him soldiers and weapons.

Then the King's son, with an army in four divisions, set forth for Takshaśilâ. The inhabitants of the town had cleared the road for the distance of two yôjanas and a half; and, bearing vessels filled with offerings, they came forth to meet him. Having advanced into his presence, they said unto him: "We are not hostile unto the King's son, nor yet unto the King; but it is the King's evil ministers who oppress us." Then entered Aśoka into Takshaśilâ, and with great pomp. In like manner he entered into the kingdom of the Svaśas. Two naked giants took refuge in his camp. They received food and began to march before him, dividing the mountains at his approach. And the Devatâs uttered these words:

"Aśoka shall be a sovereign Chakravartin,

[1] One of the three kinds of divinities, the other two being Yakshas and Nâgas.

the master of the four quarters of the earth; no man shall stand in his path. In the end the earth down to the seashore shall fall beneath his sway."

On a day it came to pass that Susîma, one of the King's sons, was returning from the garden to Pâṭaliputtra, and Khallâtaka, King Bindusâra's first minister, was coming out of Pâṭaliputtra. Susîma, with playful intention, threw his gauntlet at the minister's head. But the minister thought: "To-day he throws down his gauntlet; but when he is king, it will be the Law that he will throw down; wherefore must I take measures to prevent his becoming king. So the minister detached from the Prince's fealty five hundred councillors, saying unto them:

"Aśoka hath been appointed to be one day Chakravartin, the master of the four quarters of the earth; we must place him upon the throne."

Meanwhile the inhabitants of Takshaśilâ revolted, and Susîma, the King's son, was sent against them by his father; but he could not subdue the town.

Thereafter King Bindusâra fell sick, and he said: "Bring unto me my son Susîma, I will place him on the throne; establish Aśoka in Takshaśilâ."

But the ministers made answer: "Aśoka, the King's son, is sick."

When King Bindusâra had fallen so low that but little life remained to him, they adorned

Aśoka with all manner of ornaments and took him into the King's presence, saying: "For the nonce place Aśoka on the throne; when Susîma shall have returned from Takshaśilâ, then will we re-establish him."

But the King fell into a fury.

Then Aśoka uttered these words: "If the throne be mine by right, then let the Devatâs crown me with the royal diadem." And straightway the Devatâs placed the royal diadem upon his brow.

At the sight of this miracle, blood flowed from the mouth of King Bindusâra, and he died.

When Aśoka was established upon the throne, the news of his accession was proclaimed by the Yakshas to the height of a yôjana above the earth, while the Nâgas proclaimed it to the depth of a yôjana under the earth. These things caused Râdhagupta[1] to come forth from his retreat; and throughout the neighbourhood he heard the tidings: "The days of Bindusâra are accomplished, and Aśoka sitteth upon the throne."

At the rumour of this event Susîma, filled with wrath, hastily set forth for Pâṭaliputtra. But at the first gate of the city Aśoka stationed a naked giant, at the second another giant, at the third Râdhagupta, while at the eastern gate he himself waited. In front of the eastern gate Râdhagupta erected an elephant made of wood, while he dug a hole as big as the body of Susîma,

[1] See *post*, 'The Death of King Aśoka,' p. 122.

filled it with charcoal, and covered it with grass, over which he sprinkled dust. Then he said to Susîma: "If thou art able to slay Aśoka, then shalt thou be king."

Susîma advanced towards the eastern gate, crying: "I will fight with Aśoka."

But he fell into the hole full of burning charcoal, and there died in agony.

When Susîma had thus been put to death, his giant, named Bhadrâyudha, accompanied by a following of some thousands, entered the religious life under the law of Bhagavat[1] and became Arhat.[2]

[1] One of the Buddha's many titles.

[2] The fourth stage in the eightfold path to Nirvâṇa or Dehoiana, trodden by those who have left the universal current of creatures; as to whether or no for the first three stages they must necessarily be monks there are various opinions. After passing through the first stage, Srôta-âpanna, a being must traverse 80,000 Kalpas, at the end of which he must seven times be re-born among the Devas and among men before attaining deliverance. After traversing the second stage, Sakṛid-âgâmin, a being must pass through 60,000 Kalpas and be born once among men and once among the gods before attaining deliverance. After the 40,000 Kalpas which follow the third stage, Anâgâmin, a being is exempt from returning to the world of desire before attaining deliverance. To enter the fourth stage, that of Ârhat, a being must become a monk. An Ârhat possesses supernatural faculties, and after 20,000 Kalpas will attain deliverance. The Śrâvakas and Pratyeka-Buddhas of the fifth and sixth stages have attained to the state of Bodhi or knowledge of the Buddha. But they only possess this knowledge for themselves, they cannot impart it to others. That faculty is reserved for the perfect Buddha who has attained the seventh stage which leads to the final goal of Nirvâṇa.

## II

## THE CONVERSION OF KING ASOKA

AFTER the accession of Aśoka, his ministers disobeyed him. Wherefore he said unto them: "Cut down the flowering and the fruit-bearing trees, and preserve nought but the thorny trees."

His ministers made answer: "What is in the mind of the King? It behoveth rather to cut down the thorny trees and to preserve the flowering and the fruit-bearing trees."

Three times they disobeyed the King's command. Then in fury Aśoka drew his sword and cut off the heads of his five hundred ministers.

Another time, in the spring, when the trees are covered with flowers and fruits [sic], Aśoka, surrounded by the women of his inner apartments, was going to the garden in the eastern quarter of the city. On the way he perceived an aśoka-tree in bloom. Straightway he saluted it, thinking: "Behold a tree which beareth the same name as I."

Now, the limbs of King Aśoka were hard to the touch, wherefore the young women delighted not to caress him. The King fell asleep; and while he slept, the women of his inner apartments, in vexation of spirit, broke the branches and scattered the flowers of the aśoka-tree. On his awaking, the King beheld the broken tree and asked: "Who broke it thus?" "The women of the inner apartments," he was told. On hearing this, the King was transported with wrath. He caused the five hundred women to be surrounded with wood and burnt. The people, when they beheld the cruel deeds committed by the King, said: "The King rages, he is Chandaśoka, Aśoka the Furious."

Then the first minister, Râdhagupta, remonstrated with the King, saying: "O King, it behoveth thee not to thyself perform deeds which are unworthy of thee. Thou shouldest appoint men charged to put to death those whom the King hath condemned; they would execute the sentences pronounced by the King."

Wherefore Aśoka commanded that a man should be found to execute criminals.

Not far away, at the foot of a mountain, was a cottage inhabited by a weaver. The weaver had a son, whose name was Girika, or the Mountaineer. The child was passionate and cruel; he insulted his parents; and, when he was not fighting with boys and girls, he passed his time in killing ants, flies, mice, birds, and fish on spits and in nets. So ferocious was he that he received the name of Chanda-girika, Girika the Ferocious.

It came to pass that the King's servants found him occupied with his evil practices, and they said unto him: "Wilt thou be executioner to King Aśoka?"

The child replied: "I would fain be executioner to the whole universe."

His reply was made known unto the King, who said: "Let him be brought into my presence."

So the King's men went and said to the child: "Come, the King asketh for thee."

Chanda-girika replied: "I must first go and see my father and mother."

Then he said to his parents: "O my father and my mother, grant me your permission;[1] I am about to exercise the office of executioner to King Aśoka."

But his parents endeavoured to dissuade him from entering upon this office. Whereupon Girika deprived them both of life.

Meanwhile the King's men were asking: "Wherefore tarriest thou?"

He told them everything that had happened. Thereupon was he taken unto the King, from

[1] So far the conduct of Girika is in accordance with the Buddhist recognition of parental authority. An applicant for admission to the Buddhist order was obliged to prove that he had obtained his parents' permission to enter it.

whom he demanded that a house should be built for him.

The King therefore had a house built for him, a beautiful house, but with nought pleasant therein save the entrance, and it was called "the Pleasant Prison-house."

Then said young Girika: "Grant me a favour, O King: that whosoever entereth into this house may never leave it." To which request the King replied: "So be it."

Thereafter Chanda-girika repaired to the hermitage of Kukkuṭa-ârâma,[1] where he found the monk Bâlapandita reading a Sûtra.

"There are beings who are re-born in Hell," he was reading. "The servants of Hell seize them and stretch them out on the ground, which is all of hot molten iron, so hot that it is as one single flame; thus extended, their mouths are forced open with an iron skewer and into them are pushed balls of red-hot molten iron. These balls burn the lips of the miserable sufferers; and, after consuming the tongue, the throat, the heart, the parts in the region of the heart, and the entrails, they pass out through the body. These, O monks, are the torments of Hell."[2]

Then addressing Chanda-girika the monk bade

[1] This hermitage, which plays an important part in the Aśoka legends, was probable situated near the famous Buddhist temple at Gayâ.

[2] I have here omitted several paragraphs which describe four other forms of torture varying but slightly one from the other.

him imitate these torments. Wherefore the King's executioner began to inflict these tortures and others similar to them on the criminals who were delivered unto him.

In those days, in the city of Srâvastî was a merchant who, accompanied by his wife, traversed the great ocean. There, on the high seas, his wife, being with child, was delivered of a boy who was called Samudra, or Ocean. At length, after the lapse of twelve years, the merchant returned from his voyage; but he was captured and slain by five hundred brigands. Then Samudra, the merchant's son, entered the religious life according to the Law of Bhagavat. As he travelled through the country begging alms, he reached Pâṭaliputtra. Having dressed himself at dawn, he took his cloak [1] and his bowl [2] and went into the city to beg. There, all unweening, he came to the Pleasant Prison-house. Having crossed the threshold, he found within a dwelling horrible and hell-like. Then he wished to come out, but he was seized by Chandagirika, who said unto him: "Here must thou die."

[1] A loose robe, of dull orange colour, which covered the whole of the body except the right shoulder. As well as this cloak Buddhist monks wore two under-garments also of dull orange colour. Their heads were shaved, and they were not permitted to possess more than one change of robes.

[2] The begging-bowl of Buddhist monks is a brown earthenware vessel, in shape nearly like a soup-tureen without its cover.

The monk, realising that in the end he would have to submit, was filled with sorrow and began to weep.

Then the executioner asked: "Wherefore weepest thou thus like a child?"

The monk made answer: "I weep not for the loss of my body. I weep only because the working out of my salvation is about to be interrupted. After having reached the state of man, which it is so difficult to attain unto, and the religious life, which is the source of happiness, after having had Sâkya-sinha[1] for my master, in my misfortune, I must now renounce this happiness."

Then said the executioner: "Of his grace, hath the King granted unto me the right to put to death all those who enter here. Take courage therefore. Salvation is not for thee."

Then in his anguish the monk implored the executioner to accord unto him one month's respite. And Chanda-girika vouchsafed unto him seven nights.

Nevertheless the heart of the monk was troubled by the fear of death; his mind could not escape from the thought: "In seven days I shall have ceased to exist."

On the seventh day King Aśoka surprised a woman of the inner apartments talking to a

[1] One of Buddha's numerous names, meaning "the lion of the tribe of Śâkya."

young man, with whom she was in love. At the mere sight of it the King fell into a fury. The woman and the young man he delivered into the hands of the executioner, who with a pestle pounded them in a mortar of brass so that there remained nothing of their bodies save the bones.

Greatly moved by such a spectacle, the monk exclaimed:

"Ah! how true were the words of the great hermit, the master full of compassion, when he said that the human form is like unto a ball of moss having neither substance nor solidity!

"Where now is that charm of countenance? Where now is that beauty of the body? Woe unto this world in which fools take pleasure and delight!

"My abode in the house of the executioner hath brought me succour which shall serve me to-day as I traverse the ocean of existence."

All night long he meditated on the teaching of the Buddha, and, having broken every bond, he attained to the supreme rank of Ârhat.[1]

When day had dawned, Chanda-girika said unto him: "Monk, the night is ended; the sun hath risen: behold the hour of thy death."

"Yea," answered the monk, "the night is indeed ended, that night which for me closeth a long existence; the sun hath risen, which for

[1] See *ante*, 'Childhood and Youth of Aśoka,' p. 29, note 2.

me heraldeth the moment of supreme grace. Do as thou wilt."

"I comprehend thee not," replied Chandagirika. "Explain thy words."

Then the monk answered him in these verses:

"The awful night of error hath vanished from my soul, a night darkened by the five veils,[1] haunted by the sorrows which are like unto brigands.

"The sun of knowledge hath risen; my heart is happy in heaven, and heavenly light hath revealed unto me the true worlds as they really are.

"Behold the moment of supreme grace; now do I follow in the footsteps of the Master. This body hath lived long. Do thy will."

Straightway the pitiless, stony-hearted executioner, full of wrath and caring nought for the future life, seized the monk and threw him into an iron cauldron, containing water defiled with dirt, blood, and grease. Then beneath the cauldron he kindled a fierce fire. But, albeit the fire consumed a great mass of wood, it caused the monk no pain. The executioner would have lit it again, but the fire refused to burn. As he

[1] Probably the five skandhas of Buddhist psychology: (1) the material properties of the body; (2) the sensations; (3) abstract ideas; (4) tendencies or potentialities, of which there are no less than fifty-two divisions—three being, memory, individuality, and vitality; (5) thought or reason: cf. Rhys Davids, *Buddhism* (S.P.C.K.), pp. 90–2.

was trying to discover the cause of its not burning, the executioner beheld the monk seated with crossed legs upon a lotus; and immediately he hastened to the King to inform him of this miracle.

When the King was come with a following of many thousands, the monk, knowing that the moment to convert the King had arrived, began to display his supernatural powers. From the midst of the iron cauldron, wherein he was surrounded by water, in the eyes of the gazing crowd, he rose into the air, like unto a swan; and in the air he began to produce divers miraculous appearances; so say the verses:

"From half his body came forth water, from the other half fire; producing alternately rain and flames, he shone in the sky like unto a mountain from the summit of which streams gush forth in the midst of burning verdure."

At the sight of the monk in the sky, the King, hands clasped and amazement depicted on his countenance, addressed him eagerly and said:

"Thy form, O my friend, is like unto that of man; but thy power is divine. I cannot understand thy nature, O my Lord; by what name shall I call thee who art indeed perfection? Tell me straightway who thou art, that I may know thy majesty, and that knowing it, I may, according as it lieth in me and as a disciple, honour the greatness of thy attributes and of thy merit."

Thereupon it was borne in upon the monk that the King was destined to receive instruction, to make known the Law of Bhagavat and thereby to benefit a vast number of creatures. Therefore the monk, explaining his attributes, addressed Aśoka thus;

"O King, I am the son of the Buddha, of that being full of mercy, freed from the bonds of all guilt, the most eloquent of men. I observe the Law; I crave for no kind of existence.

"Subdued by the Hero of men who hath subdued himself, having received peace from that sage who hath attained unto perfect peace, I have been delivered from the bonds of existence by him who himself is delivered from the great terrors of the world.

"And thou, O great King, thy coming hath Bhagavat foretold when he said: 'A hundred years after I have entered into complete Nirvâṇa there shall reign in the city of Pâṭaliputtra a king named Aśoka, ruler over the four quarters of the earth, a righteous king, who shall distribute my relics and set up eighty-four thousand edicts of the Law.[1] Meanwhile, O King, thou hast

[1] The edicts were engraven in different Prākrit dialects on pillars or rocks, the wide distance of which one from the other is sufficient to show the great extent of Aśoka's empire. The pillars are at Delhi and Allahabad; the rocks at Kapur

constructed this dwelling, which is like unto Hell, wherein thousands are put to death. By the destruction thereof shalt thou give unto thy people a pledge of safety and make known unto them that thou wilt fulfil the Law of Bhagavat."

Then he uttered these words:

"O King of men, grant security unto the people who implore thy pity; satisfy the desire of the Master and multiply the edicts of the Law."

Then the King, feeling drawn unto the Law of Bhagavat, clasping his hands as a token of respect, spoke thus in order to gratify the Religious:

"O Son of the Sage, who art possessed of the ten powers,[1] forgive me this wicked deed. I confess it this day before thee; and I seek refuge with Buddha, the Ṛishi,[2] with the first of the Assemblies, with the Law proclaimed by the Aryas.[3]

"And I make this resolve: this day, filled with veneration for the Buddha and with love for him, I will adorn the earth by covering it

da Giri, near Peshaur, at Girnar in Guzerāt, at Dhauli in Orissa, and at Babra, on the road running south-west from Delhi to Jayapura." (Rhys Davids, *Buddhism* (S.P.C.K.), p. 223.)

[1] The ten supernatural powers.

[2] This title, here used to describe the Buddha, was generally applied to the sages of the older teaching, *i.e.* of Brahminism.

[3] The most eminent among the Buddha's disciples: those who have grasped the four truths, viz. (1) that sorrow exists; (2) that it is the heritage of every creature; (3)

with Châityas in honour of the chief of the Djinas;[1] and the Châityas shall be radiant as a swan's wing, as a sea-shell, yea, even as the moon.''

Meanwhile, by the exercise of his supernatural power, the Religious came forth out of the executioner's house. The King likewise was about to depart, when Chanda-girika, with clasped hands, implored him, saying:

"O King, thou hast granted unto me this favour, that a man once having entered here shall never leave this dwelling."

"What!" cried Aśoka. "Wouldest thou put me to death also?"

"Yea," replied the executioner.

Then the King called for his servants; and straightway was Chanda-girika seized by the executioners and cast into the torture-chamber, wherein he was consumed by fire. The Prison-house called Pleasant was pulled down, and security was restored to the people.

the importance of deliverance from sorrow; (4) that by knowledge alone can such deliverance be wrought. The Aryas also possess supernatural powers. (E. Burnouf, *Introduction*, p. 259.)

[1] Temples in honour of the Buddha.

## III

# THE ESTABLISHMENT OF THE LAW BY AŚOKA

DESIRING to distribute the relics of Bhagavat,[1] King Aśoka set forth at the head of an army in four divisions; and, having opened the monument, called the Stûpa[2] of the Vase, which Ajâtaśatru had set up, he took possession of the relics. Then he distributed them in the places whence they had been brought, and over each he erected a Stûpa. He did the same for the second Stûpa and likewise for them all down to the seventh Stûpa, taking away the relics in order to place them in new Stûpas.[3] Then he went unto Râma-grâma, where the Nâgas[4] took

[1] The bones of the Buddha.

[2] A Stûpa is a temple differing from a Châitya in that the Stûpa always contains relics, whereas the Châitya may contain merely a sacred tree or an image of the Buddha (cf. E. Burnouf, *Introduction*, p. 311, and *passim*). In form the Stûpa was a cone-shaped edifice, round at the top like an umbrella.

[3] The first being the Stûpa of the Vase. These Stûpas now opened by Aśoka were the original eight Stûpas in which the bones of the Buddha had been deposited.

[4] See *ante*, 'Childhood and Youth of Aśoka,' p. 26, note.

him down into their palace and said unto him: "Here we adore this Stûpa."

Wherefore the King abstained from opening that Stûpa. And the Nâgas conducted the King out of their palace. Touching this matter there is a verse which saith:

"The eighth Stûpa is at Râma-grâma. In those days it was kept by the Nâgas, who were full of faith. 'Let not the King take the relics from this Stûpa,' said they.

"The monarch, full of faith, reflected; and then, granting what was asked of him, departed."

The King had caused to be made eighty-four thousand caskets of gold, silver, crystal, and lapis-lazuli to contain the relics. Thereafter he gave to the Yakshas[1] eighty-four thousand vases, with as many fastenings (with which to fix the lid on to the body of the vase), distributing them over the whole earth down to the sea-shore, among great towns, medium towns, and small towns, wheresoever the fortune of the inhabitants amounted to a Kôti. And in each town he set up an edict of the Law.

. . . . . .

Then the King went to the hermitage of Kukkuṭa-ârâma. There he addressed the Sthavira[2]

[1] See *ante*, 'Childhood and Youth of Aśoka,' p. 26, note.

[2] The Sthaviras were the fathers of the Buddhist religion, the elders who composed the Assembly of the Religious. They were literally the elders, the youngest among them being 120 (see Heinrich Kern. *op. cit.*, vol. ii. p. 307).

Yaśas,[1] saying: "Behold my desire: on the same day and at the same hour I wish to set up the eighty-four thousand edicts of the Law."

"So be it," replied the Sthavira. "At that time the disk of the sun will I conceal with my hand."

And the Sthavira Yaśas did as he had promised. The same day at the same hour the eighty-four thousand edicts of the Law were set up. Thus say the verses:

"Having taken from the seven ancient temples the relics of the Ṛishi,[2] the descendant of the Mauryas[3] on the same day erected throughout the world eighty-four thousand Stûpas, resplendent with the splendour of clouds in autumn.

"When King Aśoka had established eighty-four thousand edicts of the Law, he became a just king, a king according to the Law, wherefore was he called Dharmâśoka, the Aśoka of the Law. Thus saith the verse:

"The venerable Maurya, the fortunate, set up all these Stûpas for the weal of mankind. Formerly was he known throughout the land as Chaṇḍâśoka; now hath his good work won for him the name of Dharmâśoka."

[1] Yaśas was one of the Buddha's earliest disciples. The mother and wife of Yaśas were Gautama's first female followers (see *ibid.*, vol. i. p. 108).

[2] This title is here applied to Buddha.

[3] The family name of Aśoka. One of his ancestors was called Maurya because he was the possessor of several peacocks (*mayûra* or *mora*) (cf. Edmund Hardy, *op. cit.*, pp. 10 and 11).

Soon after the King had submitted to the Law of Buddha it became his custom, whenever he met the sons of Sâkya, no matter whether they were alone or in the crowd, to salute them, touching their feet with his head. The King's minister was Yaśas, who was full of faith in Bhagavat. Yaśas said unto the King: "My Lord, it is not seemly for thee thus to prostrate thyself before mendicants of all castes." For from all castes come the ascetics of Sâkya who enter the religious life.

The King answered nothing; but some time afterwards he addressed the assembly of his councillors, saying: "I wish to know the value of the heads of divers creatures. Bring unto me, thou such a head, and thou another." Then to the minister Yaśas he said: "Bring thou a human head."

When all the heads were brought, the King said unto his councillors: "Go and sell these heads for a price."

All the heads were sold save the human head, which no one wanted.

Then said the King to his minister: "If you cannot obtain money for it, then give it to whomsoever will have it." But Yaśas could find no one to take the human head.

The minister, ashamed at his failure to dispose of the head, came to the King and told him what had happened. "The heads of cows, asses, rams, gazelles, and birds," he said, "have been bought with money by one or another; but this human head is a worthless object which no one will take even for nothing."

Then the King asked of his minister: "Wherefore did no one desire the human head?"

"Because it is a despicable object," replied the minister.

"Is it that head alone which is despicable?" asked the King, "or may the same be said of all human heads?"

"It is the same with all human heads," answered Yaśas.

"What!" cried Aśoka, "is my head likewise despicable?"

But the minister was afraid and dared not utter the truth.

"Speak what is in thy heart," said the King.

Thus encouraged, the minister answered: "Yes."

Having thus made his minister confess his thoughts, the King expressed himself thus, in the following verses:

"Yea, by a sentiment of pride and delusion, fostered by beauty and power, dost thou desire to dissuade me from prostrating myself at the feet of the Religious.

"And if my head, that worthless object, which no man desireth even when he may obtain it for nothing, meet an occasion for purification and acquire some merit thereby, what is there unlawful in that?

"In the ascetics of Sâkya thou regardest nought save caste and thou beholdest not their virtues; wherefore, puffed up with pride of birth, thou forgettest in thy error both thyself and others.

"Caste may be considered when it is a question of marriage or of an invitation, but not of the Law; for the Law is concerned with virtues, and virtues have nought to do with caste.

"When a man of high birth falls into vice he is blamed by the world; wherefore when a man of low caste is virtuous should he not inspire respect?

"It is by reason of the spirit that men's bodies are despised or honoured. The spirits of Sâkyas monks should be venerated, for they have been purified by Sâkya."

. . . . . .

And the King added:

"Hast thou not heard the words of the pitying hero of the Sâkyas?—'The wise man discerneth a treasure in an object which to others is worthless.' Such are the words of the master of truth, and a slave may understand them. If I desire to keep these commandments, he is no friend of mine who endeavoureth to dissuade me from them.

"When my body, abandoned like the pieces of a sugar-cane, shall sleep on the ground, it will be powerless to salute, or to arise, or to clasp its hands as a sign of respect.

"Of what virtuous deed will this body be

capable? Therefore what boots it to attach value to a body which must end in the dust? It is worth no more than a burning house or jewels lost in the sea.

"Those who in this perishable body fail to distinguish such things as have value, ignoring the essence of things, faint when they enter the jaws of death.

"When from a vase all its best contents have been taken, the curds, the whey, the milk, the melted butter, and the fresh butter, nought remaineth save the froth; wherefore if that vase be broken, there is no great cause for complaint. Likewise is it with the body: once the good works, which give it value, are taken away, then when it perisheth is there little cause to mourn.

"But when in this world death shatters the vessel of the body of a proud man who is a stranger to good works, then doth the fire of sorrow consume his heart, as when one breaketh a vessel of curds, of which the best is utterly lost.

"Wherefore, my Lord, be not vexed when I bow before the Religious; for he who, knowing nought of himself, sayeth, 'I am the noblest,' is shrouded in the darkesss of error.

"But he who with the torch of the Sage searcheth the body, and possesseth the ten powers[1] he is a sage; for him is there no difference between the body of a prince and that of a slave.

[1] The ten supernatural powers.

"Skin, flesh, bones, head, liver, and the other organs are the same in all men. Clothes and ornaments alone constitute the superiority of one body to another.

"But that which is essential in this world may be found in a vile body, and the wise do well to honour and salute it."

Thus did King Aśoka recognise that the body is worth less than eggshells filled with balls of sand compounded with serpents' tears. Thus did he persuade himself that the benefits resulting from respect shown to monks surpass those accruing from vast domains throughout æons of time. Then he desired to adorn himself in order to honour the Stûpas of Bhagavat; then, surrounded by his ministers, he went to Kukkuṭa-ârâma. There, with his hands clasped as a sign of respect and standing in the place of honour, he inquired: "Is there another of whom the All Wise hath uttered a prophecy like unto that which he prophesied of me when (in another existence) I offered him a handful of earth?"[1]

Then Yaśas, the elder of the Assembly, answered him thus:

[1] An allusion to the virtuous action of Aśoka in another existence when the Buddha passed him. Aśoka was then a little boy, called Jaya, who with Vidjaya, another boy of his own age, was playing in the dust of the high-road. At the sight of the Buddha's perfections the boy was filled with adoration for him; and, intending to give him flour, he threw into his bowl a handful of earth.

"Yea, O King, there is another. When Bhagavat was on the point of entering complete Nirvâṇa, after he had converted the Nâga Apatâla[1] and the Châṇḍâlî Gôpâlî the potter's wife, he went to Mathurâ,[2] where he thus addressed the venerable Ânanda[3]:

"'In this city of Mathurâ, O Ânanda, one hundred years after I have entered complete Nirvâṇa, shall there be a merchant of perfumes called Gupta. This merchant shall have a son, called Upagupta,[4] who shall be the first among the interpreters of the Law and a veritable Buddha, save that he shall lack the external signs.[5] To him is it appointed, one hundred years after I have entered complete Nirvâṇa, to play the part of a Buddha. By his instruction many Religious shall destroy all the corruptions of evil and behold face to face the condition of Ârhat.'

"Now, in the mountain of Urumunda was a cavern eighteen arms' lengths in depth and twelve in width. The Sthavira Upagupta said unto those of his disciples who had fulfilled their

[1] A great dragon, very famous in legend.

[2] At Mathurâ, on the Yamung River, was a famous Buddhist monastery.

[3] Ânanda was the nephew of the Buddha and his most beloved disciple.

[4] In the Buddhist period of India it was usual to call a son by his father's name with the addition of the prefix *upa*, which means *under* or *little*; thus, Upagupta is "the under Gupta" or "the little Gupta."

[5] The thirty-two signs of physical beauty.

duties: 'Let him who by means of my instruction hath beheld face to face the condition of Arhat throw into this cavern a wand of four fingers' length'; and it came to pass that in one single day ten thousand Arhats threw the wand into the cavern."

Then the Sthavira Yaśas uttered these words: "The Chief of the world hath predicted that the glorious Upagupta, the first among the interpreters of the Law, shall fulfil the duties of a Buddha."

"Is this perfect being already in this existence," inquired the King, "or is he yet to be born?"

The Sthavira replied: "He is already born, the magnanimous Sage, who hath triumphed over corruption; and, out of compassion for the world, he dwelleth in Mount Urumunda, surrounded by a multitude of Ârhats."

And he added: "This perfect Sage, who delighteth in the ways of the All Wise, expoundeth the Law in its purity to the multitude of his disciples, leading to the city of deliverance thousands of men and gods."

Now, in those days Upagupta, surrounded by eighteen thousand Ârhats, dwelt in the hermitage of Natabhatikâ. The King, having learnt the place of his abode, summoned the multitude of his ministers and said unto them: "Let a body of elephants be equipped with chariots and riders; straightway will I repair to the mountain of Urumunda. With my own eyes will I behold the Sage Upagupta, who is delivered from all stain."

But the ministers made answer: "My Lord, it is better to send a messenger; and then the Sage who abideth in that place will himself certainly come unto the King."

"It is not for him to come to me," replied the King, "but for me to go to him." And he added: "The form of Upagupta, which is like unto that of the Master, must be of diamond and hard as the rock. Such a man would ignore the command which a King should address unto him."

Wherefore the King sent a messenger to the Sthavira Upagupta and said: "I will go myself unto the Sthavira."

Meanwhile Upagupta was thinking to himself: "If the King come hither it will be a heavy burden for the country and for the multitude of the people." Wherefore he said: "I myself will go unto the King."

Aśoka, hearing of his resolve and thinking that the Sthavira would come by water, established a service of boats between Mathurâ and Pâṭaliputtra. Then Upagupta, in order to show favour unto the King, embarked with a following of eighteen thousand Ârhats, and reached the city of Pâṭaliputtra. Thereupon the King's men announced unto him the approach of the Sthavira.

"My Lord, happy art thou. There cometh unto thee, in order to testify his loving-kindness towards thee, Upagupta, the master of thought, the pilot of instruction; he cometh on foot and surrounded by sages who have reached the shore of the ocean of existence."

At these words Aśoka, transported with joy, took from his neck a chain of pearls worth one hundred thousand suvarṇas and gave it to the bearer of these glad tidings. Then, calling the bell-ringer, he bade him ring the bell in Pâṭaliputtra in order to announce the coming of the Sthavira Upagupta, crying:

"He who renounceth poverty, which profiteth not, and desireth happiness in this world, let him come to Upagupta, the pitiful Sage, who to all creatures bringeth heaven and deliverance.

"Those who have never beheld the first among men, the Master full of mercy, the being who is self-sufficing, let them come to the Sthavira Upagupta, the noble torch of the three worlds, so like unto the Master."

When the King by the sound of the bell had spread the tidings abroad in Pâṭaliputtra and had decorated the city, he went out to the distance of two yojanas and a half to meet the Sthavira Upagupta. The way was decked with garlands of flowers and perfumed with sweet scents; all manner of instruments were played; and the King was followed by all his ministers and all the inhabitants. In the distance he saw the Sthavira Upagupta in the midst of eighteen thousand Arhats, who surrounded him on the right hand and on the left like the two crescents of the moon. No sooner had the King descried him, than, alighting from his elephant, he went on foot to the river's bank; there, standing with one foot on the bank and the other on the deck of the boat, taking in his arms the Sthavira Upagupta, he bore him to land. When he had placed him on the ground, the King fell prostrate at his feet, like a tree cut through at the roots, and kissed the feet of the Sthavira. Then, kneeling, Aśoka clasped his hands as a token of respect, and, looking at the Sthavira, he spoke thus:

"When, after triumphing over my enemies, I beheld united beneath my sway mountain and plain down to the seashore, I did not experience so great a joy as now I feel on beholding the Sthavira.

"The sight of thee increaseth twofold the love of my heart for the most excellent Law. The cleansing sight of thee maketh manifest to my eyes, although he be absent, that incomparable Being who owed everything to himself.

"Now that the all-pitiful Chief of the Jinas is entered into rest, having for the three worlds fulfilled the function of Buddha, do thou now cause to shine the light of knowledge like the sun over the perishing universe, wherein the illusions of the world confuse the sight.

"Thou, who art like unto the Master, thou, the only eye of the universe, and the first among the interpreters of the Law, be my refuge, O my Lord, and give me thy commands; straightway will I hasten, O perfect Sage, to obey thy voice."

Then said the Sthavira: "O great King, Bhagavat, the venerable Tathâgata, the perfect and complete Buddha, hath confided to me and to thee the keeping of the Law. Let us make every endeavour to preserve what the Guide of creatures hath transmitted unto us when he was in the midst of his disciples."

Then the King made answer: "Sthavira, I have obeyed the commands of Bhagavat. I have adorned the earth with beautiful Stûpas, like unto mountain tops, decorated with parasols and waving standards and enriched with precious stones; and I have multiplied the vases which contain the relics of Bhagavat. Wives, children, houses, myself, worldly possessions and treasures, all have I renounced according to the teaching of the King of the Law."

"Well done," answered the Sthavira Upagupta. "Thou hast done well to obey the behest of the Buddha. He who useth his body in the service of what is truly essential, and who employeth material objects merely to sustain life, will not mourn when his time cometh, and he will depart to the desired dwelling of the gods."

The King with great pomp introduced the

Sthavira Upagupta into his royal dwelling, took him in his arms and placed him upon the seat prepared for him.

The body of the Sthavira Upagupta was smooth and soft, as soft as a flock of cotton. The King perceived it, and, with his hands clasped as a sign of respect, he said :

" Noble being, thy limbs are soft, soft as cotton, soft as silk of Benares ; but I, unhappy that I am, have coarse skin and my body is hard to the touch."

The Sthavira replied : " It is because I presented the peerless Being with a precious and incomparable offering ; not merely the handful of earth that thou gavest unto him, O King."

" O Sthavira," replied the King, " it was because I was then a child, and, having met a peerless Being, I gave him a handful of earth ; and of that action I reap the fruit to-day."

Then the Sthavira, desiring to set the King's mind at rest, replied to him thus : " Great King, behold the excellence of the soil in which thou didst sow that dust. To that action thou owest the brilliance of thy throne and thy supreme power."

At these words the King opened his eyes wide with amazement, and summoning his ministers, said unto them : " I have obtained the empire of a Balachakravartin merely for having given a handful of earth ! Wherefore what efforts ought ye not to make, my lords, in order to honour Bhagavat ?"

Then, falling at the feet of the Sthavira, he cried: "Behold, Sthavira, this is my desire: I wish to honour all the places in which the Blessed Buddha abode. I desire to mark them with a sign to be handed down to posterity." And he uttered these words: "All places in which the Blessed Buddha abode do I desire to honour and mark with a sign for posterity."

"Well done, O great King," replied the Sthavira. "Thy desire is good. I will to-day show unto thee the places in which the Blessed Buddha dwelt."

"I will visit them, I will honour them with clasped hands, I will mark them with a sign," said Aśoka.

Then the King, having equipped an army of four divisions, took perfumes, flowers, and garlands, and set forth, accompanied by the Sthavira Upagupta.

Upagupta began by leading the King to the garden of Lumbinī.[1] Then, putting forth his right hand, he said: "In this place, O great King, was born Bhagavat." And he added: "In this place was the first monument consecrated to the honour of Buddha, whom to behold is a delight. Here, the moment after his birth, the Solitary took seven steps along the ground. Having gazed towards the four quarters of the horizon, he uttered these words: 'Lo, this is my

[1] The famous birthplace of the Buddha, not far from Kapilavastu on the Ganges.

last existence; never again shall I enter into a woman's womb.'"

Straightway Aśoka prostrated himself at the feet of the Religious. Then, rising, he clasped his hands as a sign of respect, and said, weeping: "Happy are they and virtuous are their actions who beheld the great Solitary when he came into this world and who harkened unto his pleasant voice."

Then the Sthavira, desiring to please Aśoka, said unto him: "Great King, wilt thou behold the Divinity who was present at the birth of the most eloquent among men when in this wood he entered this life and took seven steps?"

"Yea, Sthavira, I wish to see the Divinity."

Straightway the Sthavira, extending his hand towards the tree from which the Queen Mahâmâyâ[1] had gathered a branch, spoke thus and said: "Let the Divinity which resideth in that aśoka-tree, that daughter of the gods who beheld the prophet Buddha, appear here in order to increase the faith in the Law of King Aśoka."

And at that moment the Divinity appeared close by the Sthavira Upagupta, and clasping her hands said: "Sthavira, what commandest thou?"

Then the Sthavira, turning to Aśoka, said: "Behold, O great King, the Divinity who beheld Bhagavat at the moment of his birth."

[1] Mother of the Buddha.

Clasping his hands as a token of respect, the King thus addressed the Divinity:

"Didst thou behold at the moment of birth the Sage whose body was marked with the signs of beauty, whose large eyes were like unto the lotus? Didst thou hear the first words of the Hero of Men, the pleasant words which he spake in this wood?"

"Yea," made answer the Divinity, "I beheld at the moment of birth the First of Men, whose body shone like gold. I beheld him when he was taking the seven steps. I heard the words of the Master."

"Tell me, O Divinity," inquired the King, "of the spendour of Bhagavat when he came into the world."

"I cannot describe it," the goddess replied. "But judge of it by these words:

"In this system of the three worlds, wherein Indra reigneth, the earth, shining with a miraculous light, splendid as gold, and pleasant to look upon, trembled to its mountain tops and to the seashore, like unto a vessel upon the high seas."

After giving a hundred thousand suvarṇas to the people of the country, the King caused a Stûpa to be erected in the place and withdrew.

Thereafter the Sthavira Upagupta took the King to Kapilavastu; and there, putting forth his right hand, he said:

"In this place, O great King, was the Bodhisattva[1] presented to his father, King Suddhodana. At the sight of that form, which bore the thirty-two signs of a great man, Suddhodana could not turn away from him, and he fell prostrate at the feet of the Bodhisattva. Behold, O great King, the family deity, Sâkya-vardha (he who bringeth prosperity to the Sâkyas). Immediately after his birth the Bodhisattva was brought to this deity in order that he might worship him. But the deities threw themselves at the feet of the Bodhisattva. Then King Suddhodana cried: 'Lo, unto the deities themselves the child is a god.' Wherefore he received the name of Devâtideva, which being interpreted is 'a god above the gods.'

"Here, O great King, was the Bodhisattva presented to the clairvoyant Brahmans who predict the future. Here the Ṛishi Asita declared that the child would one day be a Buddha. Here, O great King, was the child confided to his nurse, Mahâ Prajâpatî. There was he taught to write, to ride the elephant and the horse, to drive a chariot, to wield the bow and arrow, the club, the goad—in short, to perform all exercises becoming his rank. Behold the hall

[1] There is some diversity of opinion as to the meaning of this term. Heinrich Kern, *op. cit.*, vol. i. p. 24, defines it as one who is destined to appear in the world as a Buddha. See also Barnett, *The Path of Light*, Introduction, p. 20: "A being . . . destined to Buddhahood is called a Bodhisattva, or 'creature of enlightenment.'"

wherein the Bodhisattva exercised. Here in this place, protected by a hundred thousand divinities, was the Bodhisattva with his sixty thousand women. Here, disgusted with the world at the sight of an old man, a sick person, and a corpse,[1] the Bodhisattva left his dwelling to retire into the forest. Here, sitting in the shade of a Jambu-tree, and detaching himself from the conditions of sin and sorrow, by means of reflection and of judgment, he attained to Dhyâna or contemplation, which is the first stage in the path to Nirvâṇa. This condition is the result of insight, it giveth satisfaction and happiness; it resembleth the state of being exempt from all imperfection. Then it was that a little after noon, at the hour of the midday repast, the shadows of the other trees were cast towards the east, while the shadow of the Jambu-tree forsook not the body of the Bodhisattva. At this sight King Śuddhodana again prostrated himself at the feet of the Bodhisattva. By this gate did the Bodhisattva, accompanied by a hundred thousand divinities, leave Kapilavastu in the middle of the night. Here the Bodhisattva delivered up his house and his ornaments to his servant Chhandaka and dismissed him. As the book sayeth:

" 'Chhandaka, having received his ornaments and his horse, was dismissed. Alone and without

[1] Sir Edwin Arnold has put this legend into verse in *The Light of Asia.*

a servant did the Hero enter into the forest, where he was about to do penance.'

"Here it was that the Bodhisattva, changing his clothes of Benares silk for a hunter's yellow garments, embraced the life of a mendicant. In this place King Bimbisâra invited the Bodhisattva to reign with him on his throne. Here he met Arâḍa and Udraka, according to the verse which saith:

"'In this hermitage there lived the Ṛishis Udraka and Arâḍa. The Bodhisattva, that protector, that Indra among men, made himself acquainted with their teaching.' Here the Bodhisattva submitted to a severe penance during six years. Wherefore saith the book:

"'The great Solitary, having submitted to a severe penance for six years, realised that such was not the true path, and abandoned such practices.'

"In this place Nandâ and Nandabalâ, the daughters of village folk, presented to the Bodhisattva an offering of milk and honey, which was multiplied miraculously into ten offerings, and of which he partook. Thus saith the book:

"'Having eaten in this place the offering of milk and of honey given unto him by Nandâ, the great Hero, the most eloquent of men, went to sit in the shade of the Bo-tree.'[1]

[1] This tree, which was to become as sacred for the Buddhist as the tree of the cross for the Christian, was a fig-tree (*Ficus religiosa*). Each Buddha had his Bo-tree. This one was at Gaya.

"Here it was that Kâlika,[1] the King of the Nâgas, came to the Bodhisattva where he was sitting near the Bo-tree, and began to sing his praises. Wherefore is it said that when, beneath the Bo-tree, in his desire for Nirvâṇa the most eloquent of men had entered the path thereto, there came to worship him Kâlika, King of the serpents."

Straightway the King, with his hands clasped as a sign of respect, prostrated himself at the feet of the Sthavira and addressed him thus: "If only I might behold that King of the Nâgas who beheld the Tathâgata when, with the vigour of a king of wild elephants, he walked in the path!"

And forthwith the King of the Nâgas, Kâlika, appearing, with hands clasped respectfully, before the Sthavira Upagupta, addressed him and said: "Sthavira, what commandest thou?"

Then the Sthavira said unto the King: "Behold, O great King, Kâlika, the King of the Nâgas, who sang the praises of Bhagavat when, seated beneath the Bo-tree he advanced in the way of salvation."

Straightway the King, with hands clasped as a sign of respect, spoke thus to Kâlika, King of the Nâgas:

"Didst thou indeed behold him whose skin shone like molten gold? Didst thou see my peerless Master whose countenance is like unto

[1] A blind dragon.

an autumn moon? Tell me what were the attributes of the Sage with the ten powers. Tell me what was the splendour of the Sugata." [1]

"I may not describe it," said the Dragon. "But judge of it by these words:

"Touched by the soul of his foot, the earth and the mountains thereof trembled in diverse manners. Lit by the light of the Sugata, which rose like the moon over the world of men, the earth appeared beautiful and more radiant than the sunbeams."

After that conversation, the King caused a Châitya to be built in the place, and then he departed.

Thereafter the Sthavira Upagupta took the King to the Bo-tree. There putting forth his hand, he said:

"In this place, O great King, the Bodhisattva, endowed with great charity, after overcoming all the powers of Mâra, [2] attained to the state of the perfect Buddha, according to the verse:

"'There, by the Bo-tree, in a few moments did the Hero of the Religious scatter the hosts of the discomfited Namuchi. There did this peerless Being attain to the noble, the supreme, and immortal state of the Buddha.'"

[1] "The well gone" or "the well arrived": "he who has left the world of becoming in order to enter Nirvâṇa" (see Barnett, *The Path of Light*, notes, p. 95).

[2] The Evil One.

Wherefore the King gave unto the Bo-tree one hundred thousand suvarṇas and caused a Châitya to be built in that place, after which he departed.

Then the Sthavira Upagupta said unto King Aśoka: "Here it was that the four great kings of Heaven offered unto Bhagavat four stone vases, from which he chose one. In this place he received the alms of a repast from the hands of two merchants, Trapusha and Bhallika. Here Bhagavat, about to go unto Benares, was praised by one Upagana."

Finally the Sthavira, having taken the King to a place called Ṛishipatana, putting forth his right hand said unto him: "Here, O great King, did Bhagavat turn the lawful wheel of the Law."

And the Sthavira uttered these words:

"In this place our Lord, in order to set a term to the revolutions of the world, caused to turn the beautiful and excellent wheel[1] which is the very Law.

"In this place he caused one thousand ascetics with platted hair to embrace the mendicant life. Here he taught the Law to King Bimbisâra. Here were its truths revealed unto this Prince, in company with eighty thousand divinities and many thousand Brahmans and householders of Magadha. Here Bhagavat taught the Law to Śakra, the Indra

[1] See *post*, p. 122, note 1, and Renan, *Nouvelles Etudes sur la Religion*, p. 67.

of the Devas. Here were the truths revealed unto this God in company with eighty thousand Devatâs. Here our Lord worked the great miracle. After passing the time of the Varsha[1] with the Devas Trâyastrimśas in order to instruct in the Law his mother, to whom he owed his days, Bhagavat came down from Heaven escorted by a multitude of gods."

Finally the Sthavira Upagupta, having taken the King to the town of Kuśinagarî, said unto him, putting forth his right hand:

"In this place, O great King, Bhagavat, having fulfilled all the duties of a Buddha, entered completely into the regions of Nirvâṇa, wherein remaineth nought of the accumulated elements of existence." And he added this verse:

"'After subjecting to the eternal Law the world with Devas and men, Yakshas and Nâgas, the great Ṛishi, the Sage, gifted with intelligence and immense compassion, entered into his rest, tranquil henceforth because there remained no beings for him to convert.'"

At these words the King fell fainting on the ground. Water was sprinkled on his countenance and he revived. When he had returned to consciousness, he gave one hundred thousand suvarṇas to the place of the Nirvâṇa, and there he set up a Châitya.

. . . . . .

[1] See *post*, p. 69, note 2.

When King Aśoka had thus given one hundred thousand suvarṇas to each of these places, to the birthplace, to the Bo-tree, to the place where the Buddha had turned the wheel of the Law, and to the place where he entered into Nirvâṇa, he bestowed especial favour upon the Bo-tree; for there Bhagavat had attained to the state of a perfect Buddha. Wherefore to this tree he sent all his most precious jewels.

The first among the wives of the King was named Tishya-rakshitâ. The Queen, beholding Aśoka's piety, thought to herself: "The King takes his pleasure with me, and yet he sends his most precious jewels to the Bo-tree!" Then she called unto her a woman of the Mâtanga caste and said to her: "Couldst thou not destroy the Bo-tree, for it is in a way my rival?" "I can," replied the woman. Then she attached a thread to the tree, which straightway began to wither away.

The King's men announced to him that the Bo-tree was withering; and they uttered these words: "The tree, beneath which was revealed to the Tathâgata[1] the world as it is, the tree under which he attained to omniscience, the Bo-tree, O King of men, is beginning to die."

At these tidings the King lost consciousness and fell to the ground; but water was sprinkled on his countenance and he revived. Then he cried, weeping: "When I beheld the trunk of

[1] A title applied equally to the twenty-five Buddhas.

the king of trees, I thought to see Svayambhu[1] himself; but if the tree of the Lord fadeth, then also shall my life wither away."

Meanwhile Tishya-rakshitâ, beholding the King troubled with grief, said unto him: "My Lord, if the Bo-tree should die, I would crown the King with happiness."

"No woman," replied the King, "but the Bo-tree alone can give me happiness. Beneath that tree Bhagavat attained to the supreme grace of perfect Buddha."

Then said Tishya-rakshitâ unto the Mâtangî woman: "Canst thou restore the Bo-tree?"

"I can," replied the woman, "if any life be left in it."

Then she untied the thread, hollowed the ground round the trunk, and in one day watered it with one thousand vessels full of milk. After a few days the tree completely revived; and the King's men hastened to tell him the good tidings.

"My Lord, happy art thou. Behold, the tree hath revived."

Transported with joy, Aśoka went to gaze on the Bo-tree. And when he had seen it, he cried: "Deeds never accomplished by Bimbisâra and the other great kings will I now perform. I will render the highest honour to the Bo-tree. With perfumed water will I wash it; on the

[1] The Buddha.

Assembly of the Aryas[1] will I bestow hospitality during the five months of the Varsha."[2]

Then the King, having summoned the herald Sarvamitra, said unto him: "I will bestow one hundred thousand suvarṇas on the Assembly of the Âryas, and I will water the Bo-tree with water from a thousand vessels. Proclaim in my name that the Religious shall be entertained by me during the five months of the Varsha."

In those days Kuṇâla,[3] who had already lost his eyes, was on the King's right hand. Without uttering a word, he put up his fingers, with the intention of announcing that he would give double. But when Kuṇâla thus by a sign increased the sum, the multitude of the people began to laugh. The King, laughing in his turn, said to Râdhagupta: "Who doubled the sum?"

"There are many," replied Râdhagupta, "who need the merit of good works. One of those doubled it."

1 The Âryas, or the Venerable Ones, who have grasped the four fundamental truths of the Law and possess the ten supernatural powers.

2 The four or five months of the rainy season, when, because of the difficulty of travelling from place to place, the Buddhist monks abandoned their wandering life to dwell with Brahmans or householders. They spent this time in teaching, meditation, and study. When the rainy season was past, they met again in the Assembly and conferred together on their meditations in retreat. The institution of the Varsha is very ancient and may have been established by the Buddha himself (see E. Burnouf, *Introduction*, p. 255).

3 The son of Aśoka. See the following chapter.

"Well," said the King, "I will bestow on the Assembly of the Âryas three hundred thousand suvarṇas, and I will water the Bo-tree with the water of a thousand vases. Let it be proclaimed in my name that the Religious shall be entertained by me during the five months of the Varsha."

Straightway Kuṇâla raised four fingers. Whereat the King in wrath said unto Râdhagupta: "Who is he, Râdhagupta, who thus striveth with me? What person is he that is so ignorant of the world?"

Beholding the King's wrath, Râdhagupta threw himself at his feet and said: "Who but the virtuous Kuṇâla could thus contend with the King of men?"

Straightway the King, turning round to the right, perceived Kuṇâla and cried:

"Sthavira, to the Assembly of the Aryas, and first to the Bo-tree, do I dedicate my royal rank, my wives, the multitude of my councillors, Kuṇâla, and my own person, reserving only my treasure. I will water the great Bo-tree with milk and with water scented with sandal-wood, with saffron and with camphor, and contained in five thousand vases of gold, of silver, of crystal, and of lapis-lazuli. I will offer unto the tree thousands of flowers. Let it be proclaimed in my name that the Religious shall be entertained by me during the five months of the Varsha." And the King spake these words:

"The prosperity of my kingdom, my wives, the multitude of my councillors, I give all, save my treasure, to the Assembly, which is as a vessel of virtues. I give myself and Kuṇâla, who aboundeth in merit."

Then the King, going out in the presence of the Assembly, . . . caused a platform to be erected on the four sides of the Bo-tree. Going up on to the platform, he watered the Tree with water from four thousand vessels. And no sooner had he watered the Tree than it became as it was in the beginning, according to the verse which saith:

"No sooner had the King of men poured the excellent water upon the Tree than it was covered with a green and tender foliage. At the sight of the green leaves which clothed it, and of its tender buds, the King and the multitude of his ministers were filled with a great joy."

When the King had watered the Bo-tree, he set himself to bring the Assembly of the Religious into his palace. Then the Sthavira Yaśas addressed him in these words: "Great King, the Assembly of the Ayras gathered here is worthy of the greatest respect. It must receive every honour." Wherefore the King himself introduced into the palace each Religious, even the least among them.

There were two Srâmaṇeras[1] who were exchanging politenesses with each other. If one gave flour to his companion, then the other did like-

[1] Ascetics.

wise; and thus they were exchanging food and sweetmeats. When the King saw them, he began to laugh.

"Behold," he said, "two Srâmaṇeras playing at children's games."

Then, when the King had introduced every member of the Assembly, he sat down in the place of honour. But at that moment the Sthavira remonstrated with him, saying: "Has not the King inadvertently committed an oversight?"

"No," replied the King. "And yet down there two Srâmaṇeras are playing at children's games; like unto little boys playing in the sand, these Srâmaṇeras play with flour, with food, and with sweetmeats."

"Enough," answered the Sthavira. "They are two Arhats giving up their portions each to the other with equal detachment."

At these words Aśoka's heart was filled with joy, and he thought: "When I have entertained these two Srâmaṇeras, I will give unto the Assembly of the Religious cloth sufficient for the clothing of its members."

The two Srâmaṇeras, having divined the King's intention, said to each other: "It behoveth us to increase his merits."

And straightway one appeared holding a tortoiseshell, while the other brought colours.

Then the King said unto them: "Srâmaṇeras, what will ye do?"

"We divined," they answered, "that the King desired to give unto the Assembly of the Religious enough cloth to clothe its members withal, and we come to dye the cloth."

"I merely had the idea, and not one word did I utter concerning it," thought the King. "Wherefore must these noble sages possess the power of reading the thoughts of men."

And straightway he prostrated himself at their feet, and said, with hands clasped as a sign of respect: "The descendant of the Mauryas, with his servants, his people, and the inhabitants of his towns, hath attained to the height of happiness and hath successfully offered his sacrifices, since virtuous beings testify their consideration of him by bringing him such gifts."

Thereafter the King said to them: "After having entertained you, I will give unto the Assembly of the Religious enough cloth to make for each monk three garments."

Wherefore, when the five months of the Varsha were past, King Aśoka gave to each Religious three garments. And when he had given four hundred thousand cloaks to the Assembly, he ransomed from the monks his lands, his wives, the multitude of his ministers, himself, and Kuṇâla his son.

His faith in the teaching of Bhagavat had continued to increase. And he set up eighty-four thousand royal edicts of the Law.

## IV

## THE EYES OF KUṆÂLA[1]

AFTER King Aśoka had set up the royal edicts, his wife Padmāvatī bore unto him a son. The child was beautiful to look upon and his eyes shone with a radiant light. When the King heard of his son's birth he was transported with joy, and he cried: "Great is my delight, my heart is filled with infinite gladness. The splendour of the Mauryas is at its zenith. Because I rule according to the Law therefore is a son born unto me. May he cause the Law to bud and to blossom." For this reason was the child called Dharma-vivardhana, which being interpreted is "expansion of the Law."[2]

Then was the babe brought unto the King,

[1] The main episode of this Eastern legend has its parallels in Western antiquity: (1) in the legend of Phaedra and Hippolytus; (2) in the story told of Constantine's son Crispus and his step-mother Fausta. See Gibbon, *Decline and Fall of the Roman Empire*, chap. xviii. (ed. Bury, vol. ii. p. 210).

[2] This was the child's official name: in legend he is known as Kuṇâla.

who, gazing upon him, was filled with rapture and exclaimed: "How pure are the beautiful eyes of the child! They are like unto a lotus-bloom in full flower."

Then said the King unto his ministers: "Unto what can you liken the eyes of this child?"

"We know no man," they replied, "with eyes like his; but in the Himavat, the King of Mountains, is a bird called Kuṇâla, with eyes which resemble those of your son."

. . . . . .

"Let a kuṇâla be brought," said the King. And straightway a kuṇâla was presented unto him. Having gazed long at the eyes of the bird to see if there were any difference between his eyes and those of his son, the King could observe none; and so he said to his ministers: "The Prince's eyes are like unto the eyes of the Kuṇâla, wherefore let him be called Kuṇâla."

The young child was confided to the care of eight nurses: two to give him the breast, two to give him milk to drink, two to wash him, and two to play with him.

One day, when he was adorned with all his ornaments, the King, holding him in his arms, began to gaze at him fondly. Then he cried: "No, not one of my sons is so beautiful as he."

Now, in those days, in the province of Gandhâra

lived a man whose name was Pushpa-bhêrôtsa. It happened that there was born to a certain householder of that province a son more beautiful than the sons of men, but less beautiful than the gods. At his birth there appeared a lake, in a basin of precious stones, filled with water of a divine fragrance; there appeared also a great garden full of flowers and fruits. Both the lake and the garden moved; and wherever the child went, there the lake and the garden appeared. Wherefore the child was named Sundara, or the Beautiful. And with the years the child grew.

Some time afterwards, Pushpa-bhêrôtsa went with the merchants of the province to the town of Pâṭaliputtra on business. Taking with him a gift for the King, he was introduced into his presence. Then, having prostrated himself at the King's feet, he offered his gift and stood before his monarch. Aśoka showed the merchants his son Kuṇâla. "Merchants," he said, "in the countries you have visited, have you ever seen a child endowed with such perfect beauty?"

The merchants, clasping their hands as a token of respect, prostrated themselves at the King's feet; and after being assured that they might speak fearlessly, they made this reply: "In our country, O King, there is a young man, named Sundara, whose beauty surpasseth that of men, but doth not equal that of the gods. At his birth appeared a moving lake in a basin of precious stones, full of water divinely fragrant and a moving garden full of flowers and fruits. Wheresoever the young man goeth there appear the lake and the garden."

At these words the King wondered greatly; and, filled with curiosity, he sent a messenger to Sundara with the following announcement: "King Aśoka desireth to come and see the young Sundara; do all that is needful and prepare to receive the King."

But the multitude was alarmed, thinking: "If the King come hither with a great escort of soldiers, serious disasters may ensue."

Wherefore a good team was harnessed to the chariot, and Sundara, provided with a necklace of a thousand pearls as a gift for the King, was sent unto Aśoka.

Having completed his journey and reached the town of Pâṭaliputtra, he took the necklace of a thousand pearls and went unto Aśoka. The King had no sooner beheld the beauty, the brilliance, the splendour, and the perfection of the young Sundara, as well as the miraculous lake and the garden, than he was overcome with amazement.

Thereafter the King, desiring to astonish the Sthavira Upagupta, took with him the young Sundara and went to the hermitage of Kukkuṭaârâma. In this garden dwelt eighteen thousand Ârhats, with Upagupta at their head, and a double number of disciples and laymen of great virtue. Having saluted the feet of the Sthavira, Sundara sat down before him to listen to the Law, which Upagupta expounded unto him.

Then the young Sundara, whose character was now fully matured, after he had listened to the Law, desired to enter the religious life.

He made known his desire unto the King, and, in the presence of the Sthavira Upagupta, he became a Religious.

After long effort and study and persistent application, he came to realise the wheel of transmigration, which beareth five marks, and which is at once movable and immovable. Then, triumphing over all the paths by which one enters the world, destroying them, diverting them, and annihilating them, he succeeded, by the destruction of all the corruptions of evil, in beholding face to face the condition of Ârhat.

Having become one of the Ârhats, freed from all attachment to the three worlds, esteeming alike a piece of gold and a handful of earth, regarding as equal the world of space and the palm of the hand, a piece of sandal-wood and the axe which cuts it, having by wisdom alone broken an eggshell, having acquired science, supernatural knowledge, and perfect wisdom, turning his back on existence, on gain, on pleasure, and on honour, he became one of those whom all the Devas, with Indra and Upendra, hail, honour, and worship.

Then in the mind of King Aśoka there arose a doubt, and he addressed to the Sthavira the following question:

"What deeds did Sundara do that he came to possess such great beauty? What deeds did he do that at his birth there should appear a moving lake in a basin of precious stones, filled with water divinely fragrant, and a great garden, blooming with flowers and fruit?"

The Sthavira Upagupta made answer:

"This Sundara, O great King, hath formerly in other existences committed and accumulated acts which have attained their completion, and the causes of which have arrived at their maturity. They have accompanied him as the light accompanies the body that produces it. Acts committed and accumulated arrive not at their maturity in the external elements of the earth, in water, in fire, or in wind. It is only in the five intellectual attributes, in the six constituent parts of the body and in the five organs of the senses, the true elements of every person, that actions committed and accumulated, the good and likewise the evil, attain to their complete maturity. Works are not destroyed, not even by hundreds of Kalpas; but when in due time they have attained their consummation, they bring forth fruits for creatures endowed with bodies.

"Once, O great King," continued the Sthavira,

"when Bhagavat had entered into complete Nirvâṇa, the venerable Mahâ Kâśyapa,[1] with a following of five hundred Religious, was traversing the provinces of Magadha. There he desired to convoke an Assembly of the Law. It happened that a poor labourer beheld this great Assembly of the Religious plunged in grief by the death of the Master, their bodies weary and covered with the dust of travel. At this sight the labourer's heart was filled with pity; and he prepared a holy bath for the Religious, which he invited them to enter. The bath was of water heated and perfumed with diverse sweet scents. The monks went down into it, and, having bathed, they washed their garments therein. Afterwards the labourer offered them food, carefully prepared; then were communicated unto him the formula of refuge and the precepts of instruction, whereupon he uttered the following prayer:

"'May I, entering the religious life under the law of Sâkya-muni himself, attain to the condition of Ârhat.'

"Understandest thou this, O great King?" inquired the Sthavira. "He who in those days and at that time was a poor labourer is the monk Sundara. Because he offered a holy bath to the Religious, therefore is he adorned with radiant beauty, therefore there appeared with him a moving lake in a basin of precious stones, filled

[1] See 'The Legend of Vîtaśoka,' and note, p. 120.

with water scented with sandal-wood,[1] and a vast moving garden filled with flowers and fruits. Because in those days he hearkened unto the formula of refuge and the precepts of instruction, therefore in this present existence hath he beheld the condition of Ârhat face to face. Thus, O great King, is there reserved for dark deeds a dark reward, for bright deeds a bright reward, for mingled deeds a mingled reward. Wherefore, O King, in this world ought man to avoid black deeds and likewise mingled deeds, and to aim only at deeds pure and white."

When the Prince Kuṇâla grew up there was given unto him for a wife a young girl named Kânchana-mâlâ.

On a day the King with his son went forth to the hermitage of Kukkuṭa. There Yaśas, the Sthavira of the Assembly, who was acquainted with five secret sciences, beheld Kuṇâla and saw that ere long he would lose his eyes. This he made known unto the King.

"Wherefore shall this come to pass," inquired the King.

"Because Kuṇâla fails to do his duty."

"Kuṇâla," said the King, "take heed to do all that the Sthavira shall command thee."

Straightway, throwing himself at the feet of

[1] The medicinal and refreshing properties of sandal-wood are frequently referred to in Buddhist legends.

the Sthavira, Kuṇâla said: "My Lord, what commandest thou?"

"Be persuaded, O Kuṇâla, that the eye is a perishable thing." Then he added these words: "It is the source of a thousand evils. Because they esteem it too highly many men commit deeds which cause them unhappiness."

Kuṇâla fell to meditating on this maxim, which was ever in his mind. Henceforth he cared for nought save peace and solitude. Seated in the heart of the palace in a lonely place, he reflected how perishable is the source of sight and the sources of all the senses.

On a day Tishya-rakshitâ, the chief wife of Aśoka, passed by and beheld Kuṇâla, who was alone. Charmed by the beauty of his eyes, she took him in her arms and said: "Beneath thy ravishing glance, at the sight of thy beautiful form and thy radiant eyes, my whole body burns like dry straw consumed by a forest fire."

At these words Kuṇâla, closing his ears with his hands, replied: "Cease to utter such guilty words in the presence of a son, for unto me you are as a mother. Renounce so perverse a passion; such a love will lead you to Hell."

But Tishya-rakshitâ, finding that she could not seduce him, said in wrath: "Since thou turnest away from me when, transported with love, I offer myself unto thee, then know, O foolish Prince, that not long hence thou shalt cease to live."

"O mother," replied Kuṇâla, "liefer would I die while persisting in my duty and remaining pure. I would not live a life which should deserve the censure of honest folk and the scorn and condemnation of the wise, a life which, by closing against me the path to Heaven, would lead to death."

Henceforth Tishya-rakshitâ thought of nothing but how to injure Kuṇâla.

It came to pass that the town of Takshaśilâ, situated in the north and under the dominion of King Aśoka, revolted. When he heard of the rebellion the King wished to go himself; but his ministers said unto him: "O King, send the Prince; he will bring back the town to its allegiance."

Wherefore the King, having summoned Kuṇâla, spake unto him these words: "My beloved son, go thou to Takshaśilâ, and subdue it."

"Yea, sire, I will go," replied Kuṇâla.

. . . . . .

Then Aśoka, having caused the town and the road to be decorated, and having sent away all the aged, the sick and the poor,[1] went up into his chariot with his son, and departed out of Pâṭaliputtra. Before returning to the city, when

[1] This incident sounds like an echo of the legend told of Siddhârtha, afterwards the Buddha, whose father, Suddhodana, when his son went forth, had the aged, the sick, and the poor driven from his path.

Aśoka parted from his son in the way, he fell upon Kuṇâla's neck, and, gazing at his eyes, he wept, saying: "Happy are those eyes, and happy is the mortal who may for ever behold the lotus-flower of the Prince's countenance."

But a Brahman, who was an astrologer, had prophesied that ere long Kuṇâla would lose his sight. Wherefore King Aśoka, who could never tire of looking upon his son's eyes, cried, when he had gazed upon them: "The eyes of the Prince are perfect; and the King's heart overflows with love for him. This day I contemplate the pure radiance of those eyes which shed happiness, and of those eyes which are destined to perish. The town whither thou goest shall be happy as Heaven itself when it beholdeth the Prince; but when he shall have lost his eyes, all hearts in that town shall be plunged in grief."

Soon the young Prince reached the neighbour, hood of Takshaśilâ. At the news of his approach-the inhabitants, having adorned the town and the highway as far out as two yôjanas and a half, went forth to meet him, bearing in their hands vessels filled with precious stones. When they had arrived before him, with hands clasped as a sign of respect, they said: "It is not against the Prince or against King Aśoka that we have rebelled; but because wicked ministers came to oppress us." Then Kuṇâla in great pomp entered into the town of Takshaśilâ.

Meanwhile King Aśoka had fallen a prey to a terrible disease. Believing it to be incurable, he commanded that Kuṇâla should be brought unto him, for he was determined to place him upon the throne. But Tishya-rakshitâ, having heard the King's command, reflected: "If Kuṇâla become king, I shall be ruined." Wherefore she said to King Aśoka: "I will undertake to cure thee, but thou must forbid any doctor to enter thy palace." The King did as Tishya-rakshitâ requested, and she restored him to health.

When the King was cured of his malady he was full of joy; and he asked Tishya-rakshitâ what he should do for her. "What gift shall I give unto you?" he inquired.

"Let the King," she replied, "grant unto me royal power for one week."

"And what shall become of me?" inquired the King.

"At the end of one week the King shall resume his power."

So Aśoka gave unto Tishya-rakshitâ royal power for one week.

The first thought of the Queen was to satisfy her hatred of Kuṇâla. In the King's name she wrote a letter commanding the inhabitants of Takshaśilâ to tear out Kuṇâla's eyes. And she added these words: "For Aśoka, a king who is strong and violent, hath commanded the inhabitants of Takshaśilâ to tear out the eyes of this enemy who is a disgrace to the house of the Mauryas."

Whenever King Aśoka issued an order which was to be executed promptly he sealed it with an ivory seal. Tishya-rakshitâ said: "I will seal this letter with the ivory seal while the King is asleep." So she went to Aśoka. But just at that moment the King awaked in terror.

"What troubleth the King?" asked the Queen.

"I have just dreamed a sad dream," he replied. "I beheld two vultures about to tear out the eyes of Kuṇâla."

"That means happiness for the Prince," said the Queen.

Then a second time the King awaked in terror. "O Queen," he said, "I have just dreamed a sad dream."

"What dream?" inquired the Queen.

"I saw Kuṇâla entering the city with long hair, long nails, and a long beard."

"That means happiness for the Prince," cried the Queen.

At length, the King having again fallen asleep, Tishya-rakshitâ sealed her letter with the ivory seal and despatched it to the town of Takshaśilâ.

Meanwhile the King in a dream beheld his teeth falling from his mouth. As soon as the day dawned, he called the soothsayers and asked them the meaning of his dreams.

"O King," replied the soothsayers, "he who dreams such dreams, he who in his sleep beholdeth his teeth decay and fall from his mouth will behold his son bereft of his eyes and will hear of his death."

At these words King Aśoka, rising hastily from his seat, and turning, with hands clasped as a sign of reverence, towards the four quarters of the horizon, began to implore the Divinity, uttering these words: "May the Divinity who is benevolent for the Preceptor, for the Law, and for the Assembly, which is the first among all assemblies, may the Ṛishis who are the first in the world protect our son Kuṇâla."

Meanwhile the Queen's letter had reached Takshaśilâ. When they read this missive the inhabitants of Takshaśilâ, both of the town and of the outlying country, who were rejoiced at the many virtues of Kuṇâla, dared not to make known unto him the cruel order contained in the letter. But, after having reflected long, they said: "The King is violent; he is passionate by nature. If he pardoneth not his own son, then most certainly will he not spare us. He who is capable of nourishing hatred towards so peaceful a Prince, who lives the life of a solitary, whose only desire is that all creatures may be fed, what will he feel towards us?"

At length they resolved to tell Kuṇâla and to give him the letter. Kuṇâla, having read it, cried: "The order must be obeyed; do what is commanded."

Then were the executioners brought and told to put out Kuṇâla's eyes. But, folding their hands as a sign of respect, they cried: "We dare not. And why? Because only he who is mad enough to rob the moon, the star of night, of its brightness can tear the eyes from your countenance."

Then the Prince took the ornaments from his head and said: "Do your duty as a reward for this gift."

But they refused, saying: "Such a deed would be the cause of great misfortune."

Then there came forth a man who was deformed and covered with eighteen spots of a repulsive colour, who offered to tear out the eyes of the Prince. He was brought to Kuṇâla.

At that moment there came into the young man's mind the words of the Sthaviras, and recalling them he said: "It was because they foresaw this misfortune that the sages who know the truth said: 'Behold how fleeting is this world, and how varying is the lot of man.' Yea, good friends and virtuous, careful of my advantage and desirous of my happiness were those great-hearted sages, and free from passion were those who taught me that Law. When I think on the frailty of all things, when I reflect on the counsels of my masters, I cease to tremble, my friends, at the thought of this suffering, for I know that my eyes are things which perish."

Then turning to the man, he said: "Come, take out one eye and put it in my hand."

The torturer began to do his work; and at that moment thousands of men lifted up their voices in lamentation, wailing: "Ah! Woe! Misery! Misfortune!"

"Lo! the moon, pure in splendour, falleth from heaven; a beautiful lotus-flower is torn from the cluster of white nymphaeas."

While the people thus lamented, the eye of Kuṇâla was torn from him and he received it in his hand, saying: "Why, coarse sphere of flesh, dost thou no longer behold the forms of earth? How mistaken and how guilty are those who are bound to thee and say, 'this is I.' Those who, seriously reflecting, come to recognise in thee an organ, elusive like a ball, pure but dependent, those alone shall be beyond the reach of misfortune."

While the Prince thus meditated on the instability of all beings he was rewarded by attaining the state of Srôta-âpatti [1] in the eyes of the assembled crowd.

Then Kuṇâla, beholding truths, said to the torturer: "Take out the other eye."

The man obeyed and placed the eye in the hand of the Prince.

[1] This is the first stage in the Buddhist path to Nirvâṇa.

At that moment, Kuṇâla, who had just lost the eyes of the flesh but in whom the eyes of knowledge were purified, uttered these words: "The eye of the flesh, which eludeth the grasp, hath been taken from me; but I have acquired the perfect and irreproachable eyes of wisdom. If I am forsaken by the King, I become the son of the great-hearted King of the Law, who names me his child.

"If I am fallen from supreme greatness, which brings with it so much vexation and grief, I have acquired the sovereignty of the Law, which destroyeth grief and sorrow."

Not long afterwards Kuṇâla knew that his suffering was the work not of his father Aśoka, but of the intrigues of Tishya-rakshitâ. At this news he said: "May the Queen Tishya-rakshitâ, who hath been the means of securing me so great an advantage, continue long in happiness, life, and power."

Meanwhile, Kânchana-mâlâ heard that the eyes of her husband, Kuṇâla, had been put out. Straightway, asserting her wifely right, she rushed through the crowd in search of Kuṇâla; and she found him sightless and bleeding. Beholding him thus, she swooned and fell to the ground. In haste the bystanders brought water and endeavoured to restore her. When she began to come to herself, weeping bitterly she cried out: "The gaze of those beautiful eyes, which I so dearly loved, was all my happiness. Now that they are cast on the ground and bereft of sight, I feel that I shall die."

Then Kuṇâla, wishing to console his wife, spoke thus: "Dry thy tears; it behoveth thee not to give way to grief. Every man receiveth the reward of the deeds he hath committed in this world." And he uttered this saying: "Recognising this world to be the fruit of actions, and beholding creatures condemned to misfortune, knowing men to be created in order that their dear ones may be torn from them, my beloved, thou oughtest not to weep."

Thereupon Kuṇâla and his wife went forth from Takshaśilâ. From the moment of his conception the Prince's body had been very delicate. Wherefore he was unable to exercise any trade; he knew only how to sing and how to play upon the vîṇâ.[1] So he went about begging his bread and sharing with his wife that which he received.

Kânchana-mâlâ and the Prince retraced their steps along the road which led to Pâṭaliputtra. Having arrived in the city, they thought it their duty to return to the abode of Aśoka. But the porter refused them admittance. They were, however, taken to the shed in which the King kept his chariots. At break of day Kuṇâla touched his vîṇâ and began to sing how

[1] The Viol.

his eyes had been put out and how the vision of truth had appeared unto him. And he uttered these words:

"The sage, who by the pure flame of knowledge beholdeth the eye and the other senses, is freed from the law of transmigration.

"If thy mind, given up to sin, be tormented by the sorrows of existence, and if thou desirest happiness in this world, hasten to renounce for ever the things of sense."

King Aśoka heard the Prince's song; and he said joyfully: "It is for me that Kuṇâla sings and plays on the vîṇâ, which I have not heard for so long. The Prince hath returned to my dwelling, but he wishes to see no one."

Then, calling one of his guards, the King said unto him: "Does not this singing sound unto you like the singing of Kuṇâla? It seemeth as if he were in trouble. That voice hath profoundly moved my soul. I am as an elephant, who having lost her young has just heard its voice. Go therefore and bring Kuṇâla unto me."

Straightway the guard went to the place where the chariots were kept. There he found Kuṇâla, eyeless and with his body parched by sun and wind. Failing to recognise him, the guard returned to Aśoka and said: "O King, this is not Kuṇâla; it is a blind beggar who with his wife is in the place where are kept the King's chariots."

Then was the King greatly troubled, and he thought: "Behold the realisation of my bad dreams; in sooth, this is Kuṇâla, whose eyes have been torn out." And Aśoka uttered these words: "According to the omens which formerly appeared unto me in a dream, there is no longer any doubt that Kuṇâla hath been bereft of his eyes."

Bursting into tears he cried: "Hasten to bring this beggar into my presence; for my heart cannot rest for thinking of the misfortune which may have fallen upon my son."

The guard, having returned to the place of chariots, said to Kuṇâla: "Whose son art thou, and what is thy name?"

"Aśoka," replied Kuṇâla, "the king who enhanceth the glory of the Mauryas, beneath whose sway the whole earth doth bow in obedience, that king is my father, and my name is Kuṇâla. But to-day am I the son of the Buddha, that descendant of the sun race, who hath established the Law."

Straightway Kuṇâla was led with his wife into the presence of King Aśoka.

Beholding Kuṇâla eyeless, his body parched by sun and wind, clothed in a wretched garment discoloured by the rain during his journey, the King, being ignorant of the crime which had been committed, gazed many times at his son, but failed to recognise him. Seeing before him nought but the form of a man, he said: "Art thou Kuṇâla?"

"Yea," replied the Prince, "I am Kuṇâla."

At these words the King swooned and fell to the ground. Thus saith the sacred word:

"Beholding the countenance of Kuṇâla, from which the eyes had been torn out, King Aśoka, distracted with grief, fell upon the ground, consumed with the fire of anguish at the sight of his son's misfortune."

Water was thrown over the King; he was raised and placed upon his throne. When he had come to himself, he clasped his son in his arms. Thus saith the sacred word:

"After a few moments, the King, having regained consciousness, threw his arms around his son's neck; and, ofttimes caressing the countenance of Kuṇâla, he lifted up his voice in complaints mingled with his sobs: 'Formerly, at the sight of those eyes, like unto those of the kuṇâla, I called my son Kuṇâla; to-day, now that those eyes are extinguished, how can I continue to call him by that name?'"

Then he said:

"Tell me, tell me, my beloved son, how this countenance with the beautiful eyes hath been bereft of its light and hath become like unto the heavens robbed of their splendour by the waning of the moon?

"The heart of that man is pitiless, O my son,

who, being impelled by the hatred of the unrighteous for the righteous who feel no hatred, hath destroyed the eyes of the best of beings, of the image of the Solitary himself. This is a cruel deed which for me is the source of many evils.

"Speak to me and delay not, O thou of the beautiful countenance. Consumed with grief at the loss of thine eyes, my body perisheth like unto a forest devoured by the lightning of the Nâgas."

Then Kuṇâla, having thrown himself at his father's feet, spoke unto him thus:

"O King, thou must not sorrow thus over an event which is past. Hast thou not heard the words of the Solitary, who saith that not even the Jinas themselves, any more than the Pratyeka Buddhas,[1] may escape from the inevitable influence of deeds?

"Like unto ordinary men they reap the fruit of the actions they have committed here below; in this world is the reward of one's deeds. How therefore can I describe that which I have suffered as the work of another. In time past, O great King, I have committed some sin, and under the influence of this sin have I returned to this world, I whose eyes have been the cause of my misfortune.

[1] Those who had attained the sixth stage in the path of knowledge, to whom there remained only one more stage, that of the perfect Buddha.

"Sword, lightning, fire, poison, birds, nothing can wound the spirit, which is unchangeable by nature; it is on the body, wherein the spirit resides, that the cruel sorrows fall which seem to devour the body as a victim."

But Aśoka, with grief-racked heart, continued thus: "Who hath bereft my son of his eyes? Who in order to commit this crime hath risked the loss of so great a treasure as life? Into my heart, consumed by the fire of sorrow, wrath enters. Tell me quickly, O my son, upon whom chastisement must descend."

At length the King learned that the crime was the work of Tishya-rakshitâ. Straightway he had the Queen summoned; and when she was come he said unto her: "Wherefore, O cruel woman, does the earth not open and engulf thee? Beneath the sword or the axe will I cause thy head to fall. I renounce thee, woman covered with crime. Unjust soul, I renounce thee as the sage renounceth fortune."

Then, gazing upon her with a countenance inflamed with the fire of wrath, he added: "Wherefore should I not break her limbs in pieces after tearing out her eyes with my sharp nails? Wherefore should I not hang her alive from the gallows? Wherefore should I not cut off her nose? Wherefore should I not take out her tongue with a razor or cause her to die by poison?"

Such were the tortures with which Tishya-rakshitâ was threatened by the King of Men.

Hearing these words, Kuṇâla the magnanimous, filled with compassion, said to his father: "It would be dishonourable for thee to put to death Tishya-rakshitâ. Respect and honour, but do not slay a woman. There is indeed no reward greater than that of magnanimity. Patience, my Lord, hath been celebrated by the Sugata."[1]

Then, throwing himself again at the feet of the King, the Prince addressed to his father these words of truth:

"O King, I feel no pain; and despite the cruelty I have suffered the fire of wrath burneth not within me. In my heart there is nought but benevolence towards my mother, who commanded my eyes to be torn out.

"In order to prove the truth of these words, may my eyes now become as they were formerly."

Hardly had he uttered these words when in the countenance of Kuṇâla his eyes appeared with all their former brilliance.

Nevertheless King Aśoka, enraged against Tishya-rakshitâ, caused her to be thrown into the place of torture, where she died by fire; and all the inhabitants of Takshaśilâ Aśoka caused to be massacred.

[1] *Sugata* and *Tathâgata* are synonymous and mean *the Master*. See Heinrich Kern, *op. cit.*, vol. i. p. 98, and *post*, 'Legend of Vîtaśoka,' p. 108 note.

Then doubt arose in the minds of the Religious; and thus did they question the venerable Sthavira Upagupta, who setteth all doubts at rest: "What deed had Kuṇâla done for his eyes to be put out?"

The Sthavira made answer:

"Attend, O venerable monks. Once in times past, at Benares, was there a certain hunter who went up into the Himavat, there to slay wild beasts. One day when he was on the mountain, in the depths of a cavern he came upon five hundred gazelles herding together; and he caught them all in a net. Then he reflected: 'If I kill them, what shall I do with so much meat?' Wherefore he put out the eyes of the gazelles. And the beasts, being unable to see, could not escape. Thus by his hand were the eyes put out of many hundred gazelles.

"What think ye of that, O monks? This hunter was Kuṇâla himself. Because he put out the eyes of many hundred gazelles, as the recompense of this deed, he hath suffered through many hundred thousand years the torments of Hell. Then, in order to complete the expiation of his sin, his eyes have been put out during five hundred human existences. But what deed had he done to deserve rebirth in a royal family, a beautiful form, and the knowledge of the sacred truths? Hearken, O venerable monks:

"Formerly, in times past, when the life of a man was forty-four thousand years, there appeared in the world a perfect Buddha, whose name was Krakuchchhanda. When he had fulfilled all the duties of a Buddha, he entered the domain of Nirvâṇa, wherein remaineth nought of the elements of existence. A King named Aśoka[1] caused to be made for him a Stûpa of four kinds of precious stones. But after the death of Aśoka his throne was occupied by a sovereign who knew not the Sacred Truth. The precious stones of the Stûpa were stolen by thieves, who left nothing but the wood and earth. The people, having assembled in this place, beheld the ruins of the Stûpa and wept. Now among the people was the son of a master craftsman. This young man asked: 'Wherefore do the people weep?' Then the people answered: 'The Stûpa of Krakuchchhanda the Buddha was made of four kinds of precious stones; now behold, it is destroyed.'—The young man rebuilt it.

"There had been formerly in this place a statue of the perfect Buddha Krakuchchhanda, which was life size. It also had been destroyed. The young man restored the statue likewise and offered up this prayer: 'May my gift be

[1] An earlier king, not the father of Kuṇâla. This Aśoka is said to have lived one hundred years after the Buddha. See *ante*, Introduction, p. 15, note.

acceptable in the eyes of such a master as Krakuchchhanda! May I not be displeasing unto him!'

"What think ye of that, O venerable monks? The son of the master craftsman was Kuṇâla himself. He it was who in those days restored the Stûpa of Krakuchchhanda, and as a reward for this deed was he born in an illustrious family. Because he restored the statue of the Buddha, therefore was he born beautiful. Because he uttered the prayer we have repeated unto you, therefore was it granted unto him to please so great a master as Śâkya-muni, the perfect Buddha, to whom Kuṇâla was acceptable, therefore unto Kuṇâla was it given to know the sacred truth.

## V

# THE LEGEND OF VÎTAŚOKA

WHEN King Aśoka had submitted to the Law of Bhagavat, he set up eighty-four thousand royal edicts of the Law; and during the five months of the Varsha he maintained three hundred thousand Religious—that is, one hundred thousand Ârhats and two hundred thousand disciples and laymen filled with virtue. The multitudes covering the earth down to the seashore were moved with devotion to the Law of Bhagavat. The brother of Aśoka, whose name was Vîtaśoka, favoured the Tîrthyas.[1] They had convinced him that deliverance is not for the Śrâmaṇeras,[2] the sons of Śâkya,[3] for they seek pleasure and flee from pain. On a day it came to pass that King Aśoka said to his brother: "It behoveth thee not to favour such things as are without

[1] Brahmanist ascetics.

[2] Sectarian ascetics.

[3] The Śâkyas were the Aryan tribe to which the Buddha belonged. Their seat was at Kapilavastu, about 100 miles north-east of Benares.

foundation; it is in the Buddha, in the Law and in the Assembly that thou shouldest believe, then would thy faith have its object in reality."

On another day King Aśoka went forth to hunt the antelope. Then Vîtaśoka beheld in the forest a Ṛishi, who, surrounded by five fires, was subjecting himself to severe mortifications. The Prince approached, and, having saluted his feet, put to him this question: "O blessed one, how long hast thou inhabited this forest?"

"Twelve years," answered the anchorite.

"And on what feedest thou?"

"On fruits and on roots."

"And with what art thou clothed withal?"

"With rags and with darbha-leaves."

"And thy bed?"

"The green grass."

"Is there aught that troubleth thee in thy penance?"

"Yea," answered the Ṛishi, "for when I behold the mating of the antelopes, then am I consumed with the fever of desire."

Whereupon Vîtaśoka lifted up his voice and cried: "If even this anchorite by a penance so severe fail to stifle passion, what will become of the Srâmaṇeras, sons of Sâkya, who desire soft seats and fine linen? How may they subdue passion?"

And he uttered these verses:

"If the Ṛishis, dwelling in the lonely forest,

living on air, on water, and on roots, by such severe austerities practised for so long be powerless to still their passions, then how may the Sâkyas control their senses, they who devour so much meat, who feed on butter, on curds, and on rice well seasoned? If such a thing were possible, then might Mount Vindhya traverse the ocean.

"Yea, King Aśoka is in very truth the dupe of the Srâmaṇeras, the sons of Śâkya, to whom he showeth respect."

Aśoka heard these words; and because his mind was full of invention, he said to his ministers: "Vîtaśoka careth for nought save for the Tîrthyas; by cunning must I bring him to regard with equal favour the Law of Bhagavat."

"Let the King command," answered the ministers.

"When I have entered into my bathroom," said the King, "after I have taken off my head-dress and my diadem, the symbols of royalty, you must by some means contrive to put the head-dress and the royal diadem on Vîtaśoka and to make him sit upon the throne."

"It shall be done," replied the ministers.

The King, I have taken off his head-dress and the royal diadem, symbols of royalty, entered into the bathroom. Then the ministers said to Vîtaśoka: "When King Aśoka shall die, you will be king; meanwhile put on these royal ornaments. We will place upon your head the head-dress and the royal diadem, and lead you to the throne; and we shall see how the royal insignia become you."

Straightway the ministers adorned Vîtaśoka with the signs of royalty and placed him upon the throne. Then they told the King. The latter, beholding Vîtaśoka wearing the head-dress and the royal diadem, symbols of royalty, and seated upon the throne, cried: "Lo! while I am still alive dost thou usurp the kingship! Holà! Come here!" And at that very moment appeared executioners wearing blue garments and long hair, and carrying in their hands a bell. Prostrating themselves at the King's feet, they said: "What doth the King command?"

"I deliver unto you Vîtaśoka," he replied.

Then, addressing the Prince, the executioners said to him: "We, the executioners, armed with the sword, we take possession of thy person."

But the ministers threw themselves at the feet of Aśoka entreating him: "Pardon, O King! Vîtaśoka is your brother."

"I will pardon him," replied Aśoka, "but for seven days only. He is my brother, and because of my love for him I grant him royalty for seven days."

Straightway there was heard the sound of hundreds of instruments; cries of "Long live the King" greeted the Prince; thousands of men assembled before him, stretching out their hands to him as a sign of respect; and hundreds of women surrounded him. But the executioners stayed at the palace gate. At the close of the first day they presented themselves before Vîtaśoka and said to him: "Behold one day past, Vîtaśoka; only six more days remain unto thee." On the second day they did the same, and the same on the following day. Finally, on the seventh, Vîtaśoka, adorned with the royal insignia, was conducted into the presence of Aśoka, who said unto him: "Vîtaśoka, what didst thou think of the singing, the dancing, and the concert of instruments?"

"I have seen nothing, neither have I heard anything," answered Vîtaśoka; and he uttered these words: "I listed not to the singing, I beheld not the dancing of the women. How can he who tasted none of these pleasures give his opinion of them?"

"Vîtaśoka," replied the King, "I granted thee royalty for seven days; hundreds of instruments have been played before thee; cries of 'Long live the King' have greeted thee; the multitude hath honoured thee, clasping their hands before thee as a token of respect; hundreds of women have served thee; how therefore canst thou say: 'I have heard nothing, I have seen nothing'?"

"No," answered Vîtaśoka; "I have neither seen the dancing nor have I heard the sound of singing; I have neither smelt the sweet odours nor have I tasted the sweet savours; the gold, the jewels, the necklace, and the forms which I touched I perceived not; the multitude of women was powerless to charm a miserable man condemned to death."

"Women, dance, song, the palace with its lounges and couches, fortune, youth, beauty, all—even earth itself with its varied treasures was empty and joyless for me as long as I beheld the blue-garbed executioners seated tranquilly at my gates.

"At the sound of the blue-garbed executioners' bell the terror of death possessed me, O chief of kings.

"Summoned by the goads of fear, I was deaf to the ravishing voices, I was blind to the dancing, I was insensible to the pangs of hunger.

"A prey to the fever of death, I knew not sleep; I passed my nights in meditating on my decease."

"Ah then," replied Aśoka, "if the fear of one death which was to deprive thee of one life alone was enough to hinder thee from tasting the delights of kingship, how thinkest thou do the Religious, horrified at the thought of that death which is to end hundreds of existences, contemplate the places where they may be reborn and the evils which await them there? In Hell, the sufferings of the body delivered to the flames;

among beasts, the terror of being devoured one by the other; among the Pretas,[1] the tortures of hunger and thirst; among men, the anxieties of hard and strenuous existence; among the gods, the fear of falling and losing happiness: behold the five causes of misery, the five chains which fetter the three worlds. Tormented by the sorrows of mind and body, the very attributes of which existence is composed are for them veritable executioners; in the organs of the senses villages made desolate; in inanimate objects brigands: in short, the whole of the three worlds devoured by the fire of instability. How then can passion find a place in their hearts?"

Then he uttered these words:

"If the fear of that death which is but to deprive thee of one life alone can so torment thee as to prevent thee from enjoying pleasant things such as rejoice the heart, what pleasure shall the heart of the Religious find in food and other objects of the senses, they who think on the terrors of death repeated throughout hundreds of existences?

"How may fine garments, beds, couches, and vases attract hearts which are set upon deliverance, which behold in such things enemies and assassins, for whom the body is as a dwelling on fire, and who regard all beings as perishable?

[1] Shades of the dead. See Heinrich Kern, *op. cit.*, vol. i. p. 377.

"Shall not deliverance be for those who desire nought else, for such as turn away from existence, for those on whose hearts the many causes of pleasure sit as lightly as doth the water on the leaves of the lotus?"

Thus by means of the King's stratagem was Vîtaśoka brought to look favourably upon the Law of Bhagavat.

Clasping his hands as a token of respect, Vîtaśoka said to the King: "My Lord, I seek refuge with the blessed Tathâgata,[1] the perfect and complete Buddha; I seek refuge with the Law and with the Assembly." And he uttered these words: "I seek refuge with him whose eyes are pure as a freshly opened lotus, with him whom the gods, the sages, and men delight to honour; I seek refuge with the pure Law of Buddha and with the Assembly."

Then Aśoka, casting himself upon his brother's neck, said: "No, I have not forsaken thee, but this means have I taken to plant in thy heart love for the Law of Bhagavat.

From that time Vîtaśoka honoured the

[1] ". . . from time to time a Tathâgata is born into the world, a fully Enlightened One, blessed and worthy, abounding in wisdom and goodness, happy, with knowledge of the world, unsurpassed as a guide to erring mortals, a teacher of gods and men, a Blessed Buddha."

Extract from the Buddhist Suttas quoted by T. W. Rhys Davids, Hibbert Lectures, *Origin and Growth of Religion*, p. 64.

Châityas of Bhagavat, offering them sweet perfumes, garlands of flowers, and causing to be played a multitude of instruments; and he hearkened unto the Law, and he showed respect unto the Assembly.

One day he repaired to the hermitage of Kukkuṭa-ârâma; there he found the Sthavira called Yaśas, who was an Arhat endowed with the six supernatural powers. Vîtaśoka sat at his feet in order to listen to the Law. The Sthavira began to consider him, and straightway he discerned that the elements of his conversion were complete, that he had attained his last existence, and that in his present body he was to realise the condition of Arhat. Wherefore the Sthavira began to praise the mendicant life in order to persuade Vîtaśoka to embrace it.

No sooner had Vîtaśoka heard the words of the Sthavira than the desire to become a mendicant under the law of Bhagavat took hold upon him. Rising to his feet, and clasping his hands as a token of respect, he spoke thus to the Sthavira: "Oh that I might embrace the religious life according to the discipline of the most renowned Law! Oh that I might obtain the investiture and become a monk! Oh that I might practise before thee the duties of a religious life!"

"Friend," replied the Sthavira, "make known thy desire unto King Aśoka."

Having gone to the place where the King was, Vîtaśoka clasped his hands as a token of respect and said: "O King, grant me thy permission; I desire to embrace the religious life according to the discipline of the most renowned Law, leaving this house in perfect faith." And he uttered these words:

"Like an elephant who knows not the goad I had gone astray; but, thanks to the powerful bit of thy intelligence, the instructions of the Buddha brought me back into the right path.

"Therefore, O sovereign master of kings, must thou grant me a favour: permit me to wear the glad signs of the perfect Law, the first among the lights of the world."

When he heard these words, Aśoka, with tears in his eyes, cast himself upon the neck of his brother and said: "Vîtaśoka, renounce this resolve. The mendicant lives and consorts with persons of low caste; he is clothed in rags gathered from the dust where slaves have thrown them; his food is begged from the hand of another, his bed and his seat are upon the grass scattered at the foot of a tree. When he is sick he must lie upon leaves, he must feed on what others have thrown away, with difficulty can he procure medicine. And thou, who art delicate, thou art unable to endure the pain of hunger, of thirst, of heat and of cold. Renounce this design, I entreat of thee."

"No, my Lord," replied Vîtaśoka, "so to do would be to act as one who craves for things; but he who desireth to embrace the religious life suffereth not the pains that it brings; he beholdeth not the enemy deprive him of power; he is not reduced to poverty. At the sight of a suffering world in the grip of death, exhausting itself in vain efforts, I feared to be born again, and I resolved to enter into the way of happiness and of safety."

At these words King Aśoka began to weep and to groan.

But Vîtaśoka, desiring to console him, uttered these words: "Since, seeing that once they have entered the ever-moving litter of the world men are condemned to fall from it, wherefore doth this emotion take hold upon thee? Are we not all destined to be separated one day?"

"Well," said Aśoka, "then begin here, in this house, to serve your noviciate to the mendicant life."

In the heart of the palace, in a tree-planted enclosure, rugs were spread for the prince upon the lawn, and there was his food brought unto him. As a mendicant he began to wander through the inner apartments; but the food given to him was good. Then the King said to the women of the inner apartments: "Give him to eat such things as are given to the begging monks." Wherefore the Prince was served with damaged and fusty meal, which he felt bound to eat. But Aśoka saw it and prevented him, saying: "Since I permit it thou mayest lead the life of a beggar; but when thou hast received alms, show them to me."

Some time afterwards Vîtaśoka went to the hermitage of Kukkuṭa-ârâma. And on the way this thought occurred to him: "If I lead the life of a mendicant in the palace, then am I in the midst of the multitude. Wherefore he withdrew into the country of the Videha [1] and there began to beg. At length, after frequent and strenuous endeavour, he attained to the rank of Ârhat. When the venerable Vîtaśoka had attained thereto he experienced the happiness and joy of deliverance, and he made this reflection: "I am in very deed an Ârhat."

The first thing he did was to go to the gates of King Aśoka.

"Go," he said to the guard, "and announce to King Aśoka that Vîtaśoka is at his gate and that he desireth to see the King."

The guard, going straightway to the King, said unto him: "O King, happiness is thine; Vîtaśoka is at thy gate and he desireth to see the King."

"Go quickly," answered the King, "and bring him in."

Straightway Vîtaśoka was brought into the

[1] The ancient Mithila, the modern Tirhut.

palace. No sooner had the King beheld his brother than, rising from the throne, he fell prostrate at the feet of the Religious, just as a tree falls when it hath been cut through at the root. Then, gazing upon the venerable Vîtaśoka, he said, weeping: "Although he seeth me, that emotion which men generally feel when they meet troubleth him not; doubtless he is filled with the savoury food of that knowledge which his rank hath procured for him."

Râdhagupta was the first minister of King Aśoka. He beheld the ragged garment of the venerable Vîtaśoka and his earthen bowl, and in the bowl rice, the alms which Lûha had given him. At the sight Râdhagupta prostrated himself at the King's feet, and, with hands clasped as a token of respect, said unto him:

"O King, since this Religious hath so few desires and is satisfied, he must assuredly have attained his end.

"What can give pleasure to one who feedeth upon alms, who is clothed in rags gathered from the dust-heaps, and whose dwelling is under the trees?

"To one whose great heart is unfettered, whose healthy body is free from disease, who disposeth of his existence as he will, in the world of men such a one beholdeth eternal feasting."

When he heard these words, joy filled the King's heart, and he cried: "As I behold delivered from pride, from arrogance, and from sorrow this scion of our race, who hath renounced the family of the Mauryas, the town of Magadha and all its precious treasures, I seem to see my capital hasten to rise purified by his glory. Expound unto us nobly the Law of the Wise and its ten powers."

Then the King, taking his brother in his arms, placed him upon the seat prepared for him; then with his own hand he gave him the food which had been made ready; and when the Religious had finished his meal, washed his hands, and put his bowl on one side, the King sat down opposite the venerable Vîtaśoka to listen to the Law.

Then the venerable Religious, desiring to instruct Aśoka by a discourse touching the Law, said unto him: "Attentively perform the duties of royalty; it is difficult to obtain the three precious objects[1]; honour them constantly, my Lord."

And when in this manner he had rejoiced the King by expounding the Law, Vîtaśoka withdrew.

But Aśoka, with hands clasped in the midst of five hundred ministers and followed by a procession of many thousand inhabitants of the town and country, who surrounded him respect-

[1] The distinguishing marks of a King of kings, of the ideal monarch or Chakka-vatti, viz. the wheel, the white elephant, and the horse. See Rhys Davids, *Indian Buddhism*, Hibbert Lectures, 1881, pp. 131–7.

fully, set forth to follow the venerable Vîtaśoka. Thus said the word:

"The brother is followed by the King, his elder, who reverently accompanies him; such is the visible result, and one worthy to be celebrated, of the adoption of the religious life."

Then the venerable Vîtaśoka, desiring to give an idea of his merit in the sight of the multitude, by means of his supernatural power rose into the air. And King Aśoka, clasping his hands as a sign of veneration and surrounded by hundreds of thousands of his people, kept his eyes fixed upon the sky; and gazing at the venerable Vîtaśoka, he uttered these words:

"Freed from all family attachment, like a bird thou soarest away, leaving us enchained by the bonds of man's craving for pleasure.

"This power which is made manifest in the sage, who is filled with peace and self-control, is the fruit of contemplation, fruit not revealed unto men who are blinded by desire.

"This supreme supernatural power covers us with shame, for we are swollen with the pride of life; this intelligence causes us to hang our heads, for we are puffed up with the satisfaction of our own wisdom.

"This sage, who hath attained his end, alarms us, for we in our blindness believed that we had received our reward; and now a cloud of tears obscureth our gaze, for in reality we are not free."

Meanwhile the venerable Vîtaśoka went into the country beyond the frontier, and there set up his seat and made his bed. In that place a serious sickness befell him. King Aśoka, having heard of it, sent him medicine and servants. Then was the head of the Religious, through his sickness, covered with leprosy; but when the sickness departed his hair grew again, and he sent back the medicine and the servants. He began to eat chiefly such food as contained milk, wherefore he repaired to a cow-bier in the neighbourhood, where he lived as a mendicant.

About this time there arrived in the town of Puṇḍra-vardhana a man who was the devotee of the Brahmanist mendicants; at the feet of a Buddhist mendicant he overturned and broke a statue of the Buddha. A faithful Buddhist told the King, who straightway commanded that this man should be brought before him. The Yakshas heard this command a yôjana away in the sky, and the Nâgas a yôjana away underground, wherefore at that very moment the guilty man was brought before the King. At the sight of him Aśoka was filled with wrath and cried: "Let all the dwellers in Puṇḍra-vardhana be put to death." According to this command, in one single day eighteen thousand inhabitants suffered death.

Some time afterwards, at Pâṭaliputtra, another devotee of the Brahmans overthrew a statue of the Buddha at the feet of a Brahmanist mendicant, who broke it in pieces. The King, having heard of it, went in fury to the houses of the mendicant, of the devotee, and of their friends and kinsfolk, and caused all to be consumed by fire. Then he proclaimed this decree: "He who bringeth unto me the head of a Brahmanist mendicant shall receive a dînâra[1] as his reward."

Meanwhile the venerable Vîtaśoka had withdrawn for a night into a shepherd's hut. He was again sick; his garments were in rags; his hair, his beard, and his nails had grown to an extraordinary length. The shepherd's wife thought to herself: "This must be some Brahmanist mendicant who hath entered our hut to pass the night." Wherefore she said to her husband: "Son of my master, lo, here is an opportunity to earn a dînâra; let us slay this monk, and take his head to King Aśoka." Straightway the shepherd drew his sword from its sheath and approached Vîtaśoka. This venerable Religious was possessed of the knowledge of what had previously happened to him. He saw that he was on the eve of reaping the fruit of deeds done long ago. Wherefore, convinced in his own heart, he remained perfectly still. The shepherd

[1] The denarius is a Western coin of somewhat late introduction into India. The reference to it points to the late date of the Aśoka legend.

cut off his head with his sword, and carried it to King Aśoka, saying: "Give me a dînâra."

The King beheld the head and thought he recognised it. Nevertheless the thin hair agreed not with the resemblance he sought. The doctors and the servants were summoned. On seeing it, they said: "My Lord, this is the head of Vîtaśoka."

At these words the King fell fainting on the ground. Water was sprinkled on his face and he was restored to consciousness. Then his ministers said unto him: "Thy commands, O King, have brought down misfortune on the head of a sage who was delivered from passion; revoke thy commands and restore security to thy people."

Wherefore the King restored peace unto his people by forbidding that henceforth any man should be put to death.

Meanwhile the Religious, who were perplexed with doubts, approached the venerable Upagupta, who resolveth all doubt, and questioned him thus: "What deed had the venerable Vîtaśoka committed thus to merit death by the sword?"

"Hearken, venerable persons," replied the Sthavira, "to the deeds he committed in previous existences. Once in times long past, O Religious, there lived a hunter who supported himself by killing antelopes. In the forest was a spring on the border of which the hunter stretched his nets and set his traps. There it was that he killed the antelope. When there are no Buddhas in the world, then are born Pratyeka Buddhas.[1] Now, a certain Pratyeka Buddha, having gone down to the spring to eat, came up and went to sit with crossed legs beneath a tree. Scenting his presence from afar, the antelopes came not down to the spring. When the hunter arrived he saw that the game had not visited the spring as usual; then step by step he reached the place where the Pratyeka Buddha was seated. As he beheld him, this idea came into the hunter's mind: 'This is he who hath driven away my beasts'; and drawing his sword from its sheath, he slew the Pratyeka Buddha.

"Ye must understand, O venerable persons, that the hunter was Vîtaśoka. Because he had once slain antelopes he was attacked by a terrible disease. Because he had slain the Pratyeka Buddha with his sword he suffered as the result of that deed the torments of Hell for many

[1] "There were two kinds of Buddhas, or men of insight; firstly, those who have seen through things and being free from delusions . . . are completely, so to speak, out of the jungle, and in the open. But they cannot trace back the several parts of the path by which they have themselves escaped, so as to be able to guide others along it. They are Pratyeka Buddhas—that is, enlightened only for one. . . . Only at rare intervals, once and again in hundreds of ages, does 'a very Buddha,' one who has the insight and can also make others see, appear in the world, and happy are they who meet him" (T. W. Rhys Davids, *Indian Buddhism*, Hibbert Lectures, 1881, p. 146).

thousand years; for five hundred years among men was he born and born again, his life ever being cut short by the sword; at length, albeit he had attained to the rank of Ârhat, he must needs perish by the sword."

"But," asked the Religious, "what deed had he done that he should be born again in an illustrious family and attain to the rank of Ârhat?"

The Sthavira replied: "In the days of Kâśyapa,[1] the perfect Buddha, was a certain Pradâna-Ruchi who entered the religious life. Thanks to him, generous donors bestowed their liberality on giving food to the Assembly, providing it with savoury drinks prepared from meat, or inviting it to their houses. Thanks to him, the Stûpas were covered with canopies, and in their honour flags, standards, perfumes, and flowers were offered and concerts were performed. In reward for these actions was he born into a family of high rank. At length, after having fulfilled the duties of a religious life for ten thousand years, he gave expression to a virtuous desire, by reason of which he attained to the dignity of Ârhat"

[1] According to Tibetan tradition, Kâśyapa compiled the third great collection of Buddhist books, the *Abhidharma* (E. Burnouf, *Buddhisme Indien*, p. 39). Kâśyapa lived in the days when the existence of creatures was twenty thousand years. Endowed with knowledge, he directed man like a young bull; he was preceptor of men and gods, a Blessed Buddha. He withdrew to Benares and there took up his abode (*ibid.*, p. 244).

## VI

## THE DEATH OF KING ASOKA, OR, THE GIFT OF A HANDFUL OF EARTH[1]

"WHO is that devotee of the Law of Bhagavat who hath given most alms?" inquired King Aśoka of the Religious.

"It is Anâtha-piṇḍika, the steward of thy household," answered the Religious.

"What is the sum of the alms which he hath given?" asked the King.

"One hundred kôṭis."

This reply caused Aśoka to reflect: "Lo!" he said to himself, "a steward of my household hath given one hundred kôṭis to the Law of Bhagavat!" Then he said aloud: "And I also, I will give one hundred kôṭis."

As we have seen, he had established eighty-four thousand edicts of the Law. He gave two thousand suvarṇas to each place where the edicts were set up, and he did as much for the birth-place of Sâkya-muni, for the place where he had

[1] By the second title this legend is usually known.

become a Buddha, for the place where he had made the wheel [1] to turn, and for the place where he had entered into complete Nirvâṇa. He received the Religious during the five months of the Varsha, and on this occasion he gave four hundred thousand suvarṇas. He supported three hundred thousand Religious—that is, one hundred thousand Ârhats and two hundred thousand disciples and ordinary virtuous persons. He dedicated to the Assembly of the Âryas the lands of his women, the multitude of his ministers, Kuṇâla himself, reserving his treasure, however; and all these possessions he reserved for four hundred thousand suvarṇas. In this manner he gave ninety-six thousand kôtis to the Law of Bhagavat. Then he fell into a decline. "Soon shall I cease to be," he said. And this idea threw him into despair.

Râdhagupta [2] was the King's minister. He it was with whom (in one of his previous existences) he had given to Sâkya a handful of earth.[3] Be-

[1] One of the seven royal treasures possessed by Sâkyamuni. It appeared to him when he had purified himself and gone into the upper story of his palace to keep the sacred day. It was first the wheel of conquest, rolling on to the very extremities of the world, causing kings to submit to the King of kings; then the wheel of truth, set rolling in the first discourse of the Buddha and never to be turned back (Rhys Davids, Lectures on the *Origin and Growth of Religion*, Hibbert Lectures, 1881, pp. 131, 132, 138).

[2] See *ante*, 'Childhood and Youth of Aśoka,' p. 28.

[3] See *ante*, p. 56.

holding the despair of the King, Râdhagupta prostrated himself before him, and said, with hands clasped as a token of respect: "Wherefore, my Lord, do tears bathe that countenance which thy powerful enemies dare not regard and from which hundreds of lotus-eyed women cannot turn away?"

"Râdhagupta," answered the King, "I weep not for the loss of my treasures, nor for the loss of my royal rank, nor for the sorrow of departing from the world; I weep because I am about to be parted from the Âryas.

"No more shall I behold the Assembly in which reside all virtues, which is venerated alike by gods and by men; no more shall I honour it with offerings of food and refreshing drinks: this thought it is that causeth my tears to flow.

"Then, Râdhagupta, my desire was to give one hundred kôtis for the Law of Bhagavat; this desire have I not fulfilled."

Having thus spoken, Aśoka said to himself: "I will collect four more kôṭis in order to complete my alms." And straightway he began to send gold and silver to the hermitage of Kukkuṭa-ârâma."

In those days the heir-presumptive was Sampadî, the son of Kuṇâla. The ministers said unto him: "Prince, King Aśoka hath not long to live, and lo! he sendeth all his treasures to Kukkuṭa-ârâma. Now, other sovereigns possess great wealth, wherefore we ought not to let the King ruin himself."

Therefore the young prince forbade the treasurer to give money to the King.

It was the custom to give the King to eat in golden vessels. Having eaten, Aśoka began to send these vessels to Kukkuṭa-ârâma. Wherefore instead of in vessels of gold his food was served to him in vessels of silver, but these likewise the King sent to Kukkuṭa-ârâma. The silver vessels were then replaced by vessels of iron, but these also the King sent to the hermitage. Finally his food was brought to him in earthen vessels. Then, holding in his hand half an âmalaka, Aśoka summoned his ministers and his subjects, and addressed them sadly, saying: "Who now is King of this country?"

The ministers, rising from their seats, with hands clasped as a token of reverence, approached Aśoka and said: "It is thou, my Lord, thou who art King of this country."

But Aśoka, his eyes dim with a mist of tears, spake unto his ministers and said:

'Wherefore out of kindness say ye unto me that which is not true? I have fallen from royalty; there remaineth unto me nought of which I may dispose as Sovereign save the half of this fruit.

"Shame on so poor a power, which is like unto the movement of waters in a swollen river, since despite my empire over mankind I am powerless to escape from misery.

"But who may flatter himself that he can bring to nought the words of Bhagavat: 'All happiness endeth in misfortune'? In sooth he spoke not deceitful words, Gautama who lieth never.

"After uniting the whole earth beneath his sway, after suppressing war and disorder, and destroying the host of his enemies, who were puffed up with pride, after consoling the poor and wretched, King Aśoka hath fallen from glory, and now he passeth his days in misery. As, when it is cut from the plant, the flower or the leaf fadeth, so withereth away King Aśoka."

Then the King, calling to a man who was in his presence, spoke unto him and said: "Friend, though I be fallen from power, because of my former merits execute this my last command. Take this half âmalaka which is mine, go thou to the hermitage of Kukkuṭa-ârâma and present it to the Assembly. Then, prostrating thyself in my name at the feet of the Assembly, speak unto it thus and say: 'Behold to what is now reduced the wealth of the sovereign monarch of Jambudvîpa: this is his last alms; eat this fruit in such a manner that it may be distributed among the whole Assembly on which it is bestowed.'"

And the King opened his mouth and spake these words:

"Behold, to-day do I offer my last alms; my

royalty and my power have departed from me; deprived of health, of physicians, and of medicine, I have no helper save the Assembly of the Âryas.

"Eat, therefore, this fruit in such a manner that my last alms may be distributed among the whole Assembly, for such is the wish of him who offers it."

"It shall be done as thou desirest," said the man. And, taking the half âmalaka he went to the hermitage of Kukkuṭa-ârâma. There, advancing to the place of honour, with hands clasped reverently, he offered the fruit to the Assembly, uttering these words: "He who once commanded the earth united beneath his sway, and like unto the sun was the light of the world, having attained unto his zenith, beheld his prosperity stand still; his works betrayed him; and now, like unto the sun at the decline of day, is he fallen from power."

Bowing his head reverently before the Assembly, he offered unto it the half âmalaka, the visible sign of fortune's instability.

Then the Elder of the Assembly opened his mouth and spake thus to the Religious:

"To-day, O venerable persons, is it given unto you to suffer sorrow; and wherefore? Because Bhagavat hath said: 'For another's sorrow is it meet that man should be afflicted.' And what man having a heart shall not be afflicted to-day?

"Aśoka, the hero of the Mauryas, that monarch

who is a model of generosity, after being the only sovereign of Jambudvîpa, to-day possesseth nought save the half of an âmalaka !

"Now, deprived of power by his subjects, he giveth this half fruit, revealing thus his thoughts to the common folk who are puffed up with the pride of life and of pleasure."

Thereafter was the fruit pealed, and being pounded to a pulp it was distributed to the Assembly.

Meanwhile King Aśoka said unto Râdhagupta : "Tell me, beloved, who is now the Sovereign of the land ?"

Then Râdhagupta, casting himself at Aśoka's feet, with hands clasped as a token of respect, said : "My Lord, thou art the Sovereign of the land."

At these words, Aśoka, rising slightly and extending his clasped hands reverently in the direction of the Assembly, said : "To-day give I unto the Assembly of the disciples of Bhagavat the whole of this vast land down to the seashore, with the exception of my treasure." And he uttered these words :

"This land girt around by the ocean, as in a fine mantle of sapphire hue, this land enriched by mines of precious stones, this land which nourisheth all creatures and which beareth Mount Mandara, give I unto the Assembly ; may I reap the fruit of this action !

"As my reward for this good work I desire not to possess the palace of Indra, nor the world of Brahmâ; still less do I desire the happiness of royalty, for it passeth away as rapidly as flowing water.

"For the perfect faith in which I bestow this gift the reward I desire is to rule myself with a power worthy to be respected and honoured by the Âryas; such a treasure can never change."

Having recorded this gift in writing, the King gave the deed to his ministers to be sealed with the royal seal.

No sooner had he made this donation to the Assembly than he submitted to the law of time.

# THE WISDOM OF THE EAST SERIES

**Edited by L. CRANMER-BYNG and Dr. S. A. KAPADIA**

## THE SERIES AND ITS PURPOSE

THE object of the Editors of this Series is a very definite one. They desire above all things that, in their humble way, these books shall be the ambassadors of good-will and understanding between East and West—the old world of Thought and the new of Action. In this endeavour, and in their own sphere, they are but followers of the highest example in the land. They are confident that a deeper knowledge of the great ideals and lofty philosophy of Oriental thought may help to a revival of that true spirit of Charity which neither despises nor fears the nations of another creed and colour. Finally, in thanking press and public for the very cordial reception given to the "Wisdom of the East" Series, they wish to state that no pains have been spared to secure the best specialists for the treatment of the various subjects at hand.

---

### *NEW VOLUMES*

#### *In the Press*

**A CHINESE QUIETIST.** From the Mystical Philosophy of Liehtsze. Translated by LIONEL GILES, M.A. 2/- net.

#### *Just Out*

**LEGENDS OF INDIAN BUDDHISM.** Translated from "L'Introduction à l'Histoire du Buddhisme Indien" of Eugène Burnouf, with an Introduction by WINIFRED STEPHENS. 2/- net.

[*Continued over*

**THE BUSTĀN OF SADI.** From the Persian. Translated with Introduction by A. HART EDWARDS. 2/- net.

**THE RUBÁ'IYÁT OF HÁFIZ.** Translated with Introduction by SYED ABDUL MAJID, LL.D. Rendered into English Verse by L. CRANMER-BYNG. 1/- net.

**THE ALCHEMY OF HAPPINESS.** By AL GHAZZALI. Rendered into English by CLAUD FIELD. 2/- net.

**THE SINGING CARAVAN.** Some Echoes of Arabian Poetry. By HENRY BAERLEIN. 2/- net.

**THE WISDOM OF THE APOCRYPHA.** With an Introduction by C. E. LAWRENCE, Author of "Pilgrimage," etc. 2/- net.

**THE BURDEN OF ISIS.** Being the Laments of Isis and Nephthys. Translated from the Egyptian with an Introduction by JAMES TEACKLE DENNIS. 1/- net.

**THE MASTER-SINGERS OF JAPAN.** Being Verse Translations from the Japanese Poets. By CLARA A. WALSH. 2/- net.

**THE PATH OF LIGHT.** Rendered for the first time into English from the Bodhi-charyāvatāra of Śānti-Deva. A Manual of Mahā-Yāna Buddhism. By L. D. Barnett, M.A. Litt.D. 2/- net.

**THE SPLENDOUR OF GOD.** Being Extracts from the Sacred Writings of the Bahais. With Introduction by ERIC HAMMOND. 2/- net.

**A LUTE OF JADE.** Being Selections from the Classical Poets of China. Rendered with an Introduction by L. CRANMER-BYNG. 2/- net.

**THE CONFESSIONS OF AL GHAZZALI.** Translated for the first time into English by CLAUD FIELD, M.A. 1/- net.

**THE HEART OF INDIA.** Sketches in the History of Hindu Religion and Morals. By L. D. BARNETT, M.A., LITT.D., Professor of Sanskrit at University College, London. 2/- net.

**THE BOOK OF FILIAL DUTY.** Translated from the Chinese of the Hsiao Ching by IVAN CHÊN, first Secretary to the Chinese Legation. 1/- net.

**THE DIWAN OF ABU'L-ALA.** By HENRY BAERLEIN. 1/- net.

**BRAHMA-KNOWLEDGE: An Outline of the Philosophy of the Vedānta.** As set forth by the Upanishads and by Sankara. By L. D. BARNETT, M.A., LITT.D., Professor of Sanskrit at University College, London. 2/- net.

**THE CONDUCT OF LIFE; or, The Universal Order of Confucius.** A translation of one of the four Confucian Books, hitherto known as the Doctrine of the Mean. By KU HUNG MING, M.A. (Edin.). 1/- net.

**THE TEACHINGS OF ZOROASTER.** Translated with Introduction by Dr. S. A. KAPADIA, Lecturer, University College, London. 2/- net.

**THE PERSIAN MYSTICS.**

I. Jalálu'd-dín Rúmí. By F. HADLAND DAVIS. 2/- net.

II. Jámí. By F. HADLAND DAVIS. 2/- net.

**THE WAY OF THE BUDDHA.** Selections from the Buddhist texts, together with the original Pali, with Introduction by HERBERT BAYNES, M.R.A.S. 2/- net.

**THE SAYINGS OF CONFUCIUS.** A new Translation of the greater part of the Confucian Analects, with Introduction and Notes by LIONEL GILES, M.A. (Oxon.), Assistant in the Department of Oriental Books and Manuscripts of the British Museum. 2/- net.

**MUSINGS OF A CHINESE MYSTIC.** Selections from the Philosophy of Chuang Tzŭ. With Introduction by LIONEL GILES, M.A. (Oxon.), Assistant at the British Museum. 2/- net.

**THE AWAKENING OF THE SOUL.** From the Arabic of IBN TUFAIL. Translated with Introduction by PAUL BRÖNNLE, Ph.D. 1/6 net.

**THE RELIGION OF THE KORAN.** With Introduction by Sir ARTHUR N. WOLLASTON, K.C.I.E. 1/- net.

**THE WISDOM OF ISRAEL: Being Extracts from the Babylonian Talmud and Midrash Rabboth.** Translated from the Aramaic with an Introduction by EDWIN COLLINS. 1/- net.

**SA'DI'S SCROLL OF WISDOM.** By SHAIKH SA'DI. With Introduction by Sir ARTHUR N. WOLLASTON, K.C.I.E. 1/- net.
With Persian Script added. 2/- net.

**THE INSTRUCTION OF PTAH-HOTEP AND THE INSTRUCTION OF KE'GEMNI.** The Oldest Books in the World. Translated from the Egyptian with Introduction and Appendix by BATTISCOMBE G. GUNN. 1/- net.

**THE ROSE GARDEN OF SA'DI.** Selected and Rendered from the Persian with Introduction by L. CRANMER-BYNG. 1/- net.

**THE CLASSICS OF CONFUCIUS.**

I. The Book of History (Shu-King).
By W. GORN OLD. 1/- net.

II. The Book of Odes (Shi-King).
By L. CRANMER-BYNG. 1/- net.

LONDON
JOHN MURRAY, ALBEMARLE STREET, W.